PRAISE FOR
## THE LAST TRUE STORY I'LL EVER TELL

"Mr. Crawford has sifted through his memories with an eye toward resonant anecdotes and literary flourishes. . . . Crawford tells tales that bring human dimensions to his situation."
—*The New York Times*

"A tremendous book . . . incredibly gripping and incredibly well-written. . . . It's a remarkable story. . . . I commend Crawford not only for the service, but for the account of it, which is really a wonderful read, and I urge everyone to go out there and grab it."    —Jon Stewart, *The Daily Show with Jon Stewart*

"The White House wants to show the U.S. soldiers in Iraq as heroes. Critics want to show them as victims. John Crawford wants to show they are human. . . . *The Last True Story I'll Ever Tell* is a moving, harrowing, bold, and bitterly beautiful vision of the horror of war and the Americans now dying in it."
—*The Florida Times-Union*

"Now that the first wave of reporter memoirs about Iraq has reached bookstores, a second wave of accounts from soldiers has crested on the horizon. The best of the lot is certainly John Crawford's *The Last True Story I'll Ever Tell*. . . . Crawford is a wonderfully descriptive writer—and reading this book feels like climbing into a Humvee to patrol Baghdad in 130-degree heat."    —*Minneapolis Star Tribune*

*continued . . .*

"A harrowing account of daily life on the streets of Baghdad—an ordinary guy's troubles with the chain of command, bearing up under the constant threat of violence, trying to understand the nature of the military mission, and coming to terms with what it means to be a man. Crawford is lucky to survive his tour of duty, more than a year in length, but his marriage didn't. He returns to his Florida home to write this book, a tale of what he's lost. [His] bravery—and occasional foolhardiness—is never in doubt, and *The Last True Story I'll Ever Tell* takes its place among the very best tales of men at war—it rings with the raw, emotional energies of truth and anger and sadness." —*The New Orleans Times-Picayune*

"The first . . . on-the-ground memoir . . . to make an impact is *The Last True Story I'll Ever Tell*. . . . Crawford, who ended up in Iraq after joining the Florida National Guard to help pay his college tuition, turns out to be a bracing writer." —*The New York Times Book Review*

"[Crawford's] stories include accounts of raids and sandstorms; of keeping order in the long queues for rationed gasoline; of tight friendships with comrades; and tenuous relationships with local Iraqis. . . . He describes in horrendous detail two dying Iraqis whose car had been blasted by a machine-gunner from his unit. . . . [Crawford] contrasts the horror with wry observations about the foibles of officers and interpreters, and charming sketches of everyday life." —*Orlando Sentinel*

"A searing look at the stresses and failures that plague a reservist who's ripped from the comforts of home to patrol the streets of Baghdad for a year." —*Los Angeles Times Magazine*

"I picked up Crawford's book and with the first paragraph I was hooked. It's f***king dynamite. A young man pushed beyond endurance. Is a good book worth what he saw, felt, experienced? There are some bad things people know and wish they didn't. And I can just see it all: something very dark in the human heart and it cannot be vanquished. War after war. I finished the book thinking this is like Vietnam all over again. And like Michael Herr in *Dispatches*, Crawford really has it down. He's got it nailed."     —Thom Jones, author of *The Pugilist at Rest*

"Has all the immediacy of a letter from the front and none of the self-conscious polishing that can reduce military service to something akin to a hunt for 'material.'"

—*Cleveland Plain Dealer*

"A harrowing, tautly written, and ruthlessly unsentimental story of the experience that profoundly changed [John Crawford's] life."     —*St. Petersburg Times*

"*The Last True Story I'll Ever Tell* is packed with eye-witness accounts of follies, fears, frustrations, bitterness, and gutsy triumphs of American foot soldiers on the gound in the Iraqi war. [A] tell-all, rawly honest memoir."     —*Tallahassee Democrat*

"*The Last True Story I'll Ever Tell* is a savage, gritty, and compelling work that reveals the true cost of the Iraqi Adventure, the price paid by young soldiers. It's not about heroism, but about heroic endurance against the desert, the war-torn neighborhoods, and the lies of their commanders, lies that will echo the rest of their lives."     —James Crumley,
author of *One to Count Cadence*,
*The Last Good Kiss*, and *The Right Madness*

*continued . . .*

"It reminded me a little of Tim O'Brien's *The Things They Carried*, but the truth is you've never read anything quite like this before. Mr. Crawford does a beautiful job of conveying the modern infantryman's torn heart, and our nation's war literature is richer by one outstanding book. Thank you, Mr. Crawford."            —Gabe Hudson, author of *Dear Mr. President*

"Life in war-torn Iraq was raw, and Crawford's use of raw language and graphic descriptions of his life as a machine gunner in the National Guard serving in Baghdad leave readers tasting, smelling, and cringing at what it was like to be there."

—*Palatka Daily News*

"Crawford's writing pulses with urgency, and, gloriously, his story of being an American soldier in Iraq is shattering and relentless. Most chillingly for us readers in our early twenties, Crawford's story universalizes the accidental way in which this war has affected us all."

—David Amsden, author of
*Important Things That Don't Matter*

# THE LAST

AN ACCIDENTAL SOLDIER'S

# TRUE STORY

ACCOUNT OF THE WAR IN IRAQ

# I'LL EVER TELL

## JOHN CRAWFORD

RIVERHEAD BOOKS

*New York*

**THE BERKLEY PUBLISHING GROUP**
Published by the Penguin Group
Penguin Group (USA) Inc.
**375 Hudson Street, New York, New York 10014, USA**
Penguin Group (Canada), 90 Eglinton Avenue East, Suite 700, Toronto, Ontario M4P 2Y3, Canada (a division of Pearson Penguin Canada Inc.)
Penguin Books Ltd, 80 Strand, London WC2R 0RL, England
Penguin Group Ireland, 25 St. Stephen's Green, Dublin 2, Ireland (a division of Penguin Books Ltd.)
Penguin Group (Australia), 250 Camberwell Road, Camberwell, Victoria 3124, Australia (a division of Pearson Australia Group Pty. Ltd.)
Penguin Books India Pvt. Ltd., 11 Community Centre, Panchsheel Park, New Delhi–110 017, India
Penguin Group (NZ), cnr Airborne and Rosedale Roads, Albany, Auckland 1310, New Zealand (a division of Pearson New Zealand Ltd.)
Penguin Books (South Africa) (Pty.) Ltd., 24 Sturdee Avenue, Rosebank, Johannesburg 2196, South Africa

Penguin Books Ltd., Registered Offices: 80 Strand, London WC2R 0RL, England

Names and identifying information of certain people depicted in this book have been changed to protect their privacy.

First Riverhead hardcover edition: August 2005
First Riverhead trade paperback edition: April 2006
Riverhead trade paperback ISBN: 1-59448-201-2

The Library of Congress has catalogued the Riverhead hardcover edition as follows:

Crawford, John.
The last true story I'll ever tell : an accidental soldier's account of the war in Iraq / John Crawford.
p.    cm.
ISBN 1-57322-314-X
1. Crawford, John.    2. Iraq war, 2003—Personal narratives, American.    I. Title.
DS79.76.C737     2005                    2005042928
956.7044'342'092—dc22
[B]

PRINTED IN THE UNITED STATES OF AMERICA

10   9   8   7   6   5   4   3   2   1

*To the soldiers who, having scouted ahead,*
*stand alone knocking the dust from their boots*
*and waiting patiently for their comrades.*

## ACKNOWLEDGMENT

*Christian Parenti,*

*It's the same in skanky oil towns the world throughout:*
*Few people will vouch for you.*

*Thanks for doing so.*

# PREFACE

TWO YEARS AGO I was a newlywed and a college student only a few classes away from graduation. The world seemed uncomplicated. Now, all I can say for sure is that I am no longer a college student, no longer illusioned by new love, and I don't feel young anymore. My quiet optimism has been replaced by something darker, a kind of hatred—of what, I cannot even grasp or imagine.

I was raised in a small town in northeast Florida. I spent my summers playing war in the swamps behind my parents' house, listening eagerly at my father's side as he told me about his war, and I yearned. I grew larger every year, filling out, my voice deepening, but this childhood ambition continued in its flimsy state of idiocy until I was called to my own war.

I had spent three years in the 101st Airborne Division and then I enrolled at Florida State University. To pay for my education, I enlisted in the Florida National Guard, what I thought was a joke of an organization willing to pay for the entire cost of my education in return for one weekend a month, two weeks a year. I continued to wonder, as all men do, how I would deal with the bear of war. I studied, loved, and continued as civilians do, in ignorance, for four years.

In my final year, with two credits left, I was sent to Kuwait, and then to Iraq. We were promised short tours, three months, six at most.

We crossed the berm the same day as the army's Third Infantry Division, leading the invasion of Iraq. When the Third Division was sent home, our National Guard unit was passed around the armed forces like a virus: the 108th Airborne, First Marine Expeditionary, 101st Airborne, and finally the Armored Division. They were all sent home, heroes of the war. Meanwhile, my unit stayed on, my soul rotting, our unit outlasted by no one in our tenure there. The Florida National Guard, forgotten, unnoticed—at one point the government even declared that we had been pulled out of Baghdad and brought home, although all around us the capital of our enemy seethed.

Baghdad had apparently been captured, our president had declared the end of the war. I watched our warriors be replaced by occupiers, peacekeepers, and still I slept every night in the dragon's den. I awoke every time it was my turn and I crossed the threshold of our perimeter into the city streets, wondering if my luck would run out as it had for my good friend when he emptied his brains into his Kevlar helmet on the side of a shit-infested street on the banks of the Tigris River.

This book is the story of a group of college students, American boys who wanted nothing to do with someone else's war. It is *our* story. The world hears war stories told by reporters and retired generals who keep extensive notebooks and journals. They carry pens as they walk, whereas I carried a machine gun.

War stories are told to those that have not experienced the worst in man. And to the listener's ears they can sound like glory and heroism. People mutter phrases like, "I don't know how you did it." And "I could never have done that." And they look at you wondering how you have changed, wondering if you have forever lost the moral dilemma associated with taking another person's life.

All we do in the army is tell stories to each other. I like that oral tradition, if you could call it that. I feel like it's the best way to tell these stories. I wrote most of the stories while in Iraq, the rest just after I returned. I hope all of these stories continue to convey the immediacy of when and where and how they were composed.

I have too many of these stories to tell, and if just a few of them get read, the ones that real people will understand, then maybe someone will know what we did here. It won't assuage the suffering inside me, inside all of us. It won't bring back anyone's son or brother or wife. It will simply make people aware, if only for one glimmering moment, of what war is really like.

As much as I feel like this book is the story of innocence not lost but stolen, of lies and blackness—a story not of the insanity of war, but of the insanity of men—I should also share a few words from my father, from a phone conversation we had about halfway through my time in Iraq. He said to me, "Son, of all the things I wanted to see you achieve, a combat infantry badge was the last. It is also the one I am most proud of you for."

*These are the times that try men's souls. The summer soldier and the sunshine patriot will, in this crisis, shrink from the service of their country; but he that stands by it now, deserves the love and thanks of man and woman.*

—THOMAS PAINE

# ONE

# EMPTY BREATH

BY THE TIME the rain began to fall, visibility was already zero. The storm had descended on us soon after sunset, and it showed no signs of relenting. Even behind our sun/wind and dust goggles, sand swirled in mini-cyclones. There was no way to escape it. It had blown in from the south, a wall of brown blotting out the sky. There was no time to prepare for it, at most a minute or two. Just long enough to lean over to the guy next to you and say, "Son of a bitch, here we go." And just like that, the perimeter disappears; the guys sitting next to you fade into brown and disappear. You're alone; no war, no home, just you and the desert. I curled into as small a bundle as I could behind my rucksack in a vain attempt to escape the storm's fury. Any exposed skin burned with the impact of millions of shards of sand and rock.

Moments before, we had been relaxing in the waning sun playing cards; someone had been reading *The Hobbit* over his Motorola radio to a bored friend alone on the perimeter. But war is such that just when you begin to forget you're in one, it always comes crashing back to remind you.

"Hey!" someone yelled as they collapsed next to me. I couldn't tell who it was even up close. His tinted goggles and head wrap concealed his face and neck. The head wraps were sold in the PX back in Kuwait for ten dollars. Some of the guys wore them despite the Yasser Arafat–like appearance it gave. I was always scared someone would mistake me for hajji in the dark and fire me up.

"What?" I yelled back, feeling my words get snatched away by the wind and stolen into the night.

"We gotta get on the line! An armored brigade is coming!" The stranger yelled back through a fog of sand.

"What?!" I had heard him that time, but now my question was concerned more with the content of his message. "Ours, right?" I asked with a smile, forgetting that my face was as covered as his.

"No! Theirs!" And with that he moved away, immediately fading into the background of tans and browns.

"Shit," I said aloud, but no one was there to hear me.

The day before, our company commander had come and

taken two of our antitank missiles in case he needed them, and now I regretted handing over mine. I was alone again. Looking around, I tried to orient myself, but I may as well have been blind. They call it brown-out. Raindrops the size of dimes made tiny explosions in the sand beneath me, and although there was still plenty of it in the air, the sand on the ground had turned into a thick mud the consistency of concrete. It stuck to my boots, weighing them down and tripping me up.

*No way any brigade is moving in this shit*, I thought, but it was little comfort. I had never been in a tanker, and I didn't know what they could and couldn't do. An image of iron monsters rumbling toward me through the darkness made me swallow hard. On the open ground, there is nothing infantrymen fear more than tanks. We were only a few days into Iraq, and already we had reached Nasiriyah, a bustling city based on an agrarian economy. Marines right up the road had been punishing the Iraqis in Nasiriyah for days, and the storm could be the perfect opportunity for the beleaguered guerrillas to break contact and move farther north to rejoin their comrades in the defense of Baghdad.

Every American perimeter I ever saw was surrounded by a high mound of dirt collectively called "the berm." (Not to be confused with the term "crossing the berm," which refers to the wall of sand piled at the southern border to inhibit American entry into Iraq.) These walls were built not so much to keep the enemy out but to keep us from getting lost and wandering across the desert. Our berm could only

have been one hundred meters from where I had been lounging before the storm. I guessed the best possible direction
and walked that way, stooped over, head facing the ground.
When walking became too difficult, I crawled, always expecting
to hit the ten-foot-high wall that marked the edges of our little keep.

My feet hit something and tangled, and I collapsed into a
pile of concertina wire that I knew had been there for days. I
had started off with it behind me, and I realized that my entire
movement had been in a large sweeping circle back to where
I had begun.

With a curse, I snatched my leg free and knelt down. I
reached into the pouch of my load-bearing vest and pulled out
my global positioning system. I'd gotten it for a Christmas gift
shortly before I left, and I was sure it was about to prove its
worth. The small LED screen glowed eerily in the gloom as it
tracked first one satellite, then two, finally three, and so on. At
the very least, I could tell if I was traveling in a straight line,
and it could tell me where I was within one meter.

The desert grinned ominously in victory as sand seeped
into the mechanisms. The screen wavered and went dark. I
wished I, too, could just turn off for the rest of the storm. My
lungs ached from the dirt I had breathed in, and I began to find
myself more and more often disabled by coughing fits.

There was nothing to do but keep walking, and finally my
foot hit uneven ground—the berm. I didn't know exactly
where I was on it, but I felt as though I had traveled too far to
the right of where I wanted to be. I made a left face and, keep-

ing one foot on the downward slope, struggled down the line. After a short but exhausting effort, I passed a group of marines manning an Avenger antiaircraft vehicle and an electric fifty-caliber machine gun and found the fighting position I had dug a few days before, ten or fifteen meters past them. Their presence was only a slight relief. The explosive tip of an Avenger would scarcely leave a burn mark on the tough Russian-made T-72 tanks looming just out of sight.

From the top of the mud-covered hill, I peered over into nothingness. Swirling winds muffled all sights and sounds, and for a brief moment I felt like I was drowning at the bottom of a raging flood. The air looked like coffee when someone stirs in too much creamer. Shaking off the urge to panic, I listened hard for the sound of vehicles.

Someone tripped over my legs, and I cried out in anger and surprise.

"What the fuck?"

"Sorry 'bout that!" The faceless body moved up next to me in the prone.

"Hey! There's a bunch of hajji tanks moving this way! One group from the north and one from the west! Keep your eyes open!" I recognized the voice of one of the non-infantry officers who were staying inside our perimeter.

"What do you guys have that can kill a tank?!"

"What!?"

"What do you have that can kill a tank?!"

*Damn, he's awfully optimistic.*

"Oh, kill a tank! Yeah, we don't have shit that can do that!"

"What?!" It was hard to hear in the storm, and having our faces covered made it even more jumbled.

"We're fucked!" I summed up. This information seemed to sink in, but it didn't comfort him any. He shook his head and got to his knees.

"I'll be back! I'm gonna find out what's going on!" I didn't bother answering; he wouldn't have been able to hear me. To tell the truth, I didn't think he would even be able to find me again.

Once again, I found myself alone. It's a terrible feeling when you're facing anything bad, let alone a few hundred Russian tanks coming your way. I looked left, then right, and fought the urge to move closer to the marines to my right or to the soldiers that I knew must be somewhere on my left. No doubt only a few meters away one of my buddies was lying there thinking the same thoughts as I was. I tried to remember who was supposed to be on my left.

*Howell or Pearson? Why can't I remember?* It was a moot point, though; when the tanks got there, it wouldn't matter whom I was with.

My pal Sellers was a tanker before he joined the infantry, and I couldn't help but remember him telling me that if a High Explosive tank round hit the berm, it would turn the sand instantly to glass, and then the shrapnel, explosion, and hundreds of pounds of glass would tear through your body. It was information I would have been happier not knowing.

*What a super way to spend your twenty-fifth birthday, John.* I stifled a laugh at the irony of it all. Boner's birthday was today too. We had exchanged gifts at first light.

He had gotten me a chocolate-covered oatmeal cookie bar from a dehydrated Meal-Ready-to-Eat, and Kreed had given me a half-dozen coffee packets. I gave Boner a pack of Marlboro Lights, one of the many that floated around inside my rucksack.

"Happy birthday, Crawford," they had said that morning, and the most depressing thing was that I was happy with the gifts. Chocolate-covered oatmeal cookie bars are becoming a rare treat in today's MREs. And Sellers and Mears had given me an Iraqi bayonet to match the one I already had. I had two nephews, after all, and you can't very well give loot to one and not the other.

The best thing was that mail had come the night before. Sitting there in the dark, I had slowly read my card through the digital green haze of night vision.

There was a muddy paw print from my dog and a letter from my wife. Next to the paw print it read, "Happy Birthday Dad."

The sand swirled in my face as I thought of the letter and began to zone out, something infantrymen learn to do from hours of lying perfectly still.

MY WIFE was there, her soft breaths moving the sheets ever so slightly. The room was neither hot nor cold, and with a sigh I rolled over and closed my eyes again. We were still two days from Belize, and the mammoth ship churned through the Caribbean with ease; only a gentle rocking suggested the expanse of crystal-blue water outside the windows. Sighing, I realized I wouldn't be going back to sleep anytime soon and decided that a refreshing walk on the deck would ease my tension.

I swung my legs onto the floor and looked back at my sleeping wife. Ringlets of her hair cascaded off the pillow in a bright crimson waterfall. I leaned over, kissed her lips, and stood to get dressed. We were both college seniors, mere months from graduation, and on our honeymoon cruise. The salty night air filled my nose with paradise as I stretched and walked down the ship. My grades had been posted the day before, and I figured I would go to the ship's computer lab and check them. What I found was an e-mail from my dad. The army had called looking for me. My unit had been alerted.

I stayed up a while longer, looking down fifty or so stories into the churning black sea that followed the ship. The music had stopped, and no one was out drinking or laughing this late. It was just me and the open water. Every so often, another ship would twinkle in the distance, its lights a fleeting reminder of life in the rest of the world. I have heard veterans from other wars claim they never understood the reasons for the conflict they were dropped into. This was not the case with me. I had studied foreign policy and cultures in college. I knew my history and my politics. I recognized the importance of Middle Eastern oil to European and Asian powers. This was a war I didn't believe in, but no one had asked my opinion. I had signed a contract, reaped the benefits of a cheap college education, and now it was time to pay it back. Two credits from graduating, recently married, and with less than a year left in my contract, I was going to Iraq.

————

ALL THIS TIME there was a rumbling slowly growing. I didn't notice it at first, but eventually I could feel it in me, like when a car in traffic has their bass up too loud and it makes your mirrors rattle.

*Diesel engines.* The thought hit me and I struggled to make out any sounds in the screeching winds. I expected to hear tracks clanking, people yelling, but only found myself searching for something I couldn't find.

My hand found the letter in my breast pocket. I'd already memorized it, but it felt good knowing it was there to look at whenever I wanted to.

"Your parents stopped in the other day. Your dad almost cries whenever he talks about you. I think it's harder on him because he was in Vietnam and he thinks of you like he did all the young soldiers he used to know. You should write him and tell him you're okay. I found a house I love in Virginia. When you get home this summer, we can go look at it. I can't wait. . . ."

The letter had continued on in this manner for some time. Some parts made me smile, others worry. It was the first mail I had received since I left Fort Stewart two months before.

*I'll be home in no time*, I promised myself. I concentrated hard, and the specter of my honeymoon resurfaced.


I HAD RETURNED to our room a little shaken, but resolved not to tell my wife. She hadn't grown up in the military and wouldn't understand it like I did, and besides, there was no use ruining her vacation. She woke up with a smile and saw me sitting on the edge of the bed, my head in my hands. I guess she thought I was worrying about the cruise. It wasn't all that the brochure had made it out to be.

"Don't stress out too much, baby. Everything can't be perfect, you know. No matter how much you plan it."

With a sigh, I leaned back and started to laugh.

"I know. I'd just like to catch a break now and then."

"Now, do you really think you're that unlucky? You got me, didn't you?" Stephanie crooned in my ear as she gently pulled me back toward her.

"Yeah, I guess you're okay sometimes." The sarcasm was strictly for show. I had been blinded by love from the moment we met.

"Uh-huh." The kisses on my neck were starting to wear me down, and I allowed myself to be pulled next to her. Warm skin touched mine, and I shivered.

"We're going to be together forever, aren't we?"

"Yeah, baby."

"Promise me, John."

"I promise. I'll always be here with you." Three weeks later, I became a liar.


THE OFFICER that was with me before came running up and again tripped bodily on my legs.

"Goddamnit!" I bellowed at him, but this time he didn't

apologize. Moving on his elbows in a low crouch, he came up to my left and screamed into my ear.

"Your second platoon just got overrun! Eleven friendlies were taken prisoner! Watch yourself, they're coming this way!" My mouth hung open behind my neck gaiter, and I struggled to comprehend what I had heard. An image of my friends lying facedown, their blood mixing with the muddy desert sand as they were slowly buried by the storm, burned my mind's eye.

I looked over at my mud-caked weapon. I fruitlessly attempted to wipe some of the grime away from the feed tray and rounds. I was pretty sure it wasn't going to fire, but just the same I reached into my saw pouches and unclasped them, preparing another four hundred or so rounds. They would just bounce off anything armored, but I damn sure was gonna bounce a shitload of them off before they got me. The least I could do was make them work for it.

I took a deep breath and coughed up some sand.

"Modern warfare my ass." I felt my lips move but couldn't hear myself. There I was with a light machine gun, no air cover, no heavy weapons, no naval gunfire. Infantry against tank, fucking World War II shit. I wasn't really excited about visiting the cradle of civilization in the first place, let alone dying there.

I lay there, glancing at my watch every so often, and for a long time nothing happened. Sometimes ten, fifteen, or even thirty minutes had passed. More often than not, the minutes crawled through the storm, and I found myself checking in intervals of two and three minutes. The storm, sensing it was getting the better of me, doubled its attack. There was no longer any doubt about whether my weapon would fire. There was no fucking way it would work. Hours had passed and still I lay on my stomach in the melee, kicking my legs out every few seconds to keep them from being buried.

Thoughts of my friends in Second Platoon swarmed my mind. I was haunted by images of them lying facedown, blood pooling around their battered corpses.

*Shit, where is everyone?* Impatience got the better of me, and slowly I crawled to my left in search of a friendly face with which to share the torture. No one was there. Defeated, I turned back to my right and went toward the Avenger team. I found them huddled together inside their small tan tents issued to all marines.

"What the hell is going on?!"

A grizzled old marine sergeant looked surprised to see me. "They said to find cover and get out of this fucking storm! Get in here, there's room!" He offered up a place in the small tent to me, and as tempting as it was, I turned it down.

"No, thanks, Sar'nt! I gotta find my platoon!" He didn't wait for me to answer, but was in a hurry to zip up the flap and escape the angry desert. I jealously pondered why the army didn't issue me a tent, but then figured that if they had I would just bitch about carrying it.

I moved blindly, weapon slung around me, hands out to my front like a blind man who has lost his cane. I wavered left and right through the perimeter until I found a cargo-back Humvee, the flaps drawn tight. I undid two clasps in the back and the canvas began writhing in the air as water hoses do in cartoons.

"Close the fucking flap!" a voice cried out in desperation.

"Who's that!? Is that you, Mears?" I stuck my head in.

"Crawford! Close the flap, man!" I crawled in and re-attached the straps. Mears groaned as my soaking-wet and mud-covered body joined his in the tight space. He was a chubby kid with glasses that made him look both younger and smarter. In the dark I could feel him recoiling from the filth that covered me. I moved about clumsily, my uniform weighed down by fifty pounds of dirt. When the clasps were tight again and the wind had ceased to blow in, I yanked my neck gaiter down and pulled up my goggles. The truck rocked back and forth like a ship at sea, and gusts of wind threatened to tear the canvas protecting us. There were metal pipes all over the bed of the Humvee, and though we were filthy, stinky, and wet, there couldn't have been a more comfortable place in the world.

When I was reasonably comfortable, I tried without much success to light a damp cigarette.

"What's up? What happened to the tanks?"

"Man, ain't nobody out there," Mears replied with disgust.

"And Second Platoon? What about them?" I continued.

"Man, you ain't gonna believe this shit. I've been monitoring the radio right here. So some captain that's with Second Platoon thinks he sees something outside the perimeter. He runs up to Head and tells him to fire some Mark 19 rounds outside the perimeter. Now, you know Head, he just fucking smiles and starts pumping shots out there. They send a patrol out, those guys almost get shot by friendlies, and the whole thing was a fucking goat herd or some shit. Meanwhile, the pogues are running around, crying and shit, yelling that they don't want to die. Their radio operator gets on, says they're overrun. . . . You get the point."

"You have got to be shitting me." I was happy that my buddies were okay, but that is a crazy bad fuckup. "So these are the guys leading us into combat, huh?" I could feel Mears shake his head in disgust next to me.

"What about POWs? Anything about that?"

"I think some maintenance company got ambushed a couple klicks down the road."

"That fucking sucks."

We were done talking. My cigarette went out on its own in my wet hands, and I tossed it away in disgust. Leaning back against the hard metal truck bed, dripping wet, with pipes digging grooves into me, I tried to make myself comfortable. Outside, all hell was breaking loose. I pulled the letter from my breast pocket and with filthy soldier hands I gingerly opened it, taking care to keep every crease perfect as I smelled the perfume on it. The paw print again made me laugh.

I missed my dog a lot. I remember wishing he were lying next to me in the Humvee. He couldn't stop either a tank or a sandstorm, but it's nice to have your dog around when you're in trouble. The Iraqis we met didn't understand; they're cat people, and Americans are dog people. That was the best reason I could think of for going to war.

I turned on a red lens flashlight and through the eerie

glow I again looked at the letter, memorizing every stroke of ink.

"I can't wait to see you again, honey. I love you so much." Had it been so long since I'd seen her? I missed her more than I thought possible. I tried to picture my wife when she wrote it, but the voice on the page was an empty breath.

# TWO

# INTO BAGHDAD

"Formation!" The word echoed through the series of large brown circus tents that dotted the desert landscape. Some dragged the word out: "Forrmaaationnn!" Others muttered it under their breath. Regardless, everyone moved. It was late April and we were back outside Nasiriyah, except this time we had been housed en masse on an Iraqi airstrip commandeered by the Air Force to fly supplies and mail to soldiers scattered throughout the Middle East. The airmen were farther up the road, in enclosed, climate-controlled shelters designed for comfort rather than utility. My company, on the other hand, slept next to where we shit and shit next to where we ate.

There just wasn't any more room for soldiers here, and within the first day or two people started getting sick.

It started with a headache—no surprise in the early-summer heat. You'd sit inside the tent and try to read or listen to the radio ignoring the throbbing, and then a sudden wave of nausea would creep up. "I . . . I'll be right back." And you'd stagger toward the open flap and into the sunlight, trailing dust and sand behind. Some made it away from the tent and toward a semblance of privacy before they collapsed, but most just dropped right outside, puking and shitting at the same time. The lucky ones got their pants down around their ankles beforehand and there they lay, face in the sand, pants around their ankles. There wasn't much to be done. Doc Ballou would give an IV every so often to keep the afflicted hydrated, and aside from that we just waited it out.

When it happened to me I actually made it to the shitter, crawling on hands and knees there under a glowing moon. Our latrines were just plywood shacks with metal barrels underneath. When the barrels were full, soldiers would pull them out, pour in fuel, and set them alight, filling the air with thick clouds of putrid black smoke. I made it there before I passed out, falling through the flimsy door onto my face. My pants hung around my boots and I lay facedown, sand filling my nose and mouth. A few guys from other units passed by, but finally someone from my company saw me and carried me off toward a tent we had set up as a pseudo leper colony for the sick.

It was in this tent that I heard the call for formation. With a groan I sat up and grabbed my top, sliding the dirt-crusted sleeves over my sweaty arms. I groaned under the weight of my weapon and slowly staggered out into the sunlight and toward a large field where we had been meeting for daily updates that usually amounted to long, drawn-out speeches that always ended the same: "I don't know what's going on, men." They were put on by the battalion commander. He and the rest of Headquarters Company had finally arrived, albeit after the invasion was over. The term in usage was "Better late than never," although in their case I would have preferred never.

These meetings always ran on the same agenda. The company would line up, make a count, and then report to the battalion commander, who, in an unveiled attempt to prove he was one of us, would then have us "bring it in" to a large semicircle around him. The length of these meetings changed, but as of yet, not the topic. "Sir, there are rumors of a follow-on mission. Is that true?"

"Men, I haven't heard anything about that. You have all done a tremendous job; just keep up the work a little longer. We'll be home soon."

"Sir, now that the First Marine Expeditionary Force is going home, shouldn't we be going as well? I mean, we were attached to them until end of mission."

"I'm working on that, men. I'll get back to you."

This was how it went. Vague answers and no one ever asked what we all were thinking. "Sir, are you fighting to get us a follow-on mission so that you and the rest of Headquarters Company can earn your combat infantry badges and you can get some leadership time in theater? Do you feel as though you missed the war and now you're going to make up for it with our blood and sweat? Are you upset because we came over, did our jobs, and are ready to go home while you did paperwork?"

No one asked, because we already knew the answer. It was as clear on his face as the disgust was on ours.

Today's speech was different.

"I just got orders today. We're not going home yet. The 101st Airborne Division is in Baghdad and they can't pull out until someone replaces them. Alpha Company, you're to be replacing a battalion of them. I'm working on getting Bravo and Charlie Companies back and they'll be joining you shortly. It's only a temporary mission. Just until Third Infantry Division can cover down on that area."

"Temporary, sir?"

"We'll be leaving when Third Infantry Division relieves us. It's just a few months. I know you're all tired and ready to go home. I'm only asking for a little bit more."

We were good soldiers, and so we sucked it up and gave just a little more.

At three the next morning, I sat with my platoon on a lonely stretch of dark tarmac waiting for a C-130 cargo plane to take me to Baghdad. Some slept uncomfortably on the blacktop; others ate the same tired old MREs we had been forcing down twice a day for nearly four months. I leaned against my rucksack, puffing nervously on a cigarette and trying to remember some of the stars from when I was a Boy Scout. None looked familiar.

"Not much longer now," someone muttered in the dark.

"Yeah, a month or two, Third ID is gonna relieve us. They don't keep National Guardsmen overseas that long. We got jobs and shit—they know that."

"Be home in time for my kid's birthday, I bet." We all feigned confidence, but there was a bad feeling going around that was hard to ignore. Some said that Private Dwight was the smartest out of us. "Fuck that pussy. I hope he gets gangrene and fucking dies," someone said from somewhere behind me. Dwight, stressed out, tired, or just plain scared, had shot himself in the foot a few months earlier and was now back in the States, taking classes at Florida State University, drinking cold beer and banging hot sorority girls.

"I hate that fucking cunt!" We all did.

Seven hours and a few hundred kilometers later, I found myself standing up in the back of a five-ton truck, eyeing our new compound in the center of Iraq's biggest city. The Tigris River flowed behind me and ten-foot concrete walls loomed to my front. We sat uncomfortably in the trucks while the battalion commander sorted things out. The 101st wasn't expecting us; no one was.

The colonel had jumped at the opportunity to add to his résumé. It was rumored that he had brought us there without going through the proper channels. We had, more or less, just shown up. The motif wouldn't change. When we finally did go home, we left in much the same way—showing up at the airport all but unannounced.

The compound we had arrived in had until very recently been occupied by the now decimated Republican Guard. In the center was an elaborate officers' club. The locals told us that it had been a favorite hangout of Uday, the more infamous son of Saddam. During the long boring days, he had evidently passed the time by looking out through large windows at the bustling street. At the sight of a passing schoolgirl, wife, harlot, or mother that he found interesting, his soldiers would rush out and abduct her. The girl would be gang-raped. There were few formal complaints. Not only was the fear of retaliation very real, but rape is oftentimes viewed as a disgrace on the victims as well as the transgressor in certain Muslim communities. Young girls on their way to school, husbands and fathers unable to help them: Even in the heat, the thought made me shiver.

We had so far spent months in the desert and gotten just south of Baghdad before redeploying. The sudden introduction of a city was mind-blowing. The labyrinth of alleys and streets that would later become commonplace now seemed unfathomable. Enemies were behind every corner and in every window, their dark eyes plotting our demise. It was the smell that was the worst. Rotting flesh and feces permeated the air, creating a stench that was unbearable.

We were housed in a series of small apartments, equivalent to small studio apartments you might find in the most rundown of American neighborhoods. In each one a squad of nine men lived. In these cramped quarters, we seethed. There was no power, and with the coming of May the real summer heat began. We slept naked on the floor, a full bottle of water sitting next to each one of us. Puddles of sweat pooled out several feet from our bodies. There was a constant battle against the sun to stay hydrated.

The soldiers we were relieving eyed us conspicuously, and although they treated us with respect, there was no doubt that they considered us to be second class. On patrol they did their best to wear us down, and when we refused to show our weariness, they only increased the pace. They would turn through the myriad of alleyways, walking us in circles, mind-fucking us. We were all beaten down physically, but there was no way we could concede victory to them.

After a few days, the soldiers from 187th Infantry Regiment, realizing that we were infantrymen of the same caliber as they, began to teach us in earnest about the area we were patrolling. They introduced us to the people they knew in the city, told us where the trouble areas were and where never to get caught at night.

"Sometimes I'll go to the bottom of the overpass and stand there while my squad hides out behind that wall," one squad leader told me with a crazy look in his eyes. "We'll wait till someone shoots at me and then they'll take him." I offered to allow him that opportunity right then. Looking up at the sky, he politely declined with a shake of his head.

"Not the right time of day."

I smiled, and he continued walking.

"Hey, man, you know he's not shitting you, right?" a fellow machine gunner from the 101st said to me when we halted a little while later.

"Check out his body armor. Son of a bitch took a hit to the chest doing that. I saw it. Fucking nuts." Sure enough, the next time the squad leader turned around I noticed a hole in the fabric surrounding his ceramic-plated vest. I whistled in jealousy. While the armor they wore would stop a round from an AK-47, the ones we wore were antiquated relics from Vietnam that did little more than make us sweat.

We patrolled in this manner with the 101st for a week or so, and then, as promised, they left—except Third ID didn't come to relieve us. When Third ID arrived, they told us we couldn't go home yet, that we were needed desperately by them, and that when they redeployed to the States we would be able to tag along. We were part of them now.

The worst part of being an attachment is that there is no loyalty or friendliness between the units. Third ID didn't give a shit about us, or we them. We were put on a water and food ration. No supplies came our way, and soon we began commandeering civilian vehicles, our Humvees all being broken. Without a supply chain, the equipment we needed to perform our mission fell into disarray. Our night-vision devices were useless without the swing arm to mount them. Our retooled Vietnam-era rifles began to show their age, falling apart with the slightest usage. We became shadows of the shock-and-awe troops that Americans saw on television. My uniforms were torn beyond repair and my boots had no soles on them. Still we walked on, day and night, sloshing through the sewage-filled streets.

"Men, Baghdad is no more dangerous than any other city. Right now all we're dealing with is criminals. Frankly, I'd feel safer walking the streets of Baghdad than downtown Miami." That's what the battalion commander had told us. But he never did walk the streets of Baghdad, and the sounds of explosions and machine-gun fire sounded nothing like the Miami I knew. We were there to do a job, though, and regardless of how bleak it looked, we persevered.

A few days after we arrived in Baghdad, Sergeant Washington and I found ourselves at Observation Post 1, overlooking the Tigris River. As the sun started to rise, I was struck by the fact that we were there in the cradle of civilization.

"How funny is this, man? How many armies do you think have sat right here and seen this same sunrise?" Washington just nodded his head. His baby was growing up too fast, and I think he felt bad that he might be missing too many of the good parts.

I pulled out my tin canteen cup and placed it over a heat tab to make coffee. The smell of stale Maxwell House filled my nose as the steam began to rise. When it was ready, I stirred it with my finger, licked off the bitter taste, and then stood up and looked over the edge.

"Drinking coffee, watching the sun rise over the Tigris River on a beautiful spring morning. Doesn't get any better than this, right?" The smile on my face and the bitter sarcasm in my voice got Wash's attention, and he looked over the edge with me.

High clouds lit up red and orange as the first rays of sunlight broke the horizon and a slight breeze cooled our faces, causing the palm trees to dance slightly in the dawn.

"It really is awful pretty, you know?"

A whistling screech broke the morning silence as a sniper's bullet flew inches from our heads. It slammed into a piece of sheet metal we had erected as a makeshift shelter from the heat. The sound of metal clanging into metal reverberated in our ears, and we dove to the ground. Hot coffee spilled over my front.

"Motherfucker!" I stayed down, feeling it cool beneath my body.

"Fucking bullshit, man!" whispered Wash as we tasted the dust on the top of the building. How many other soldiers over the centuries had tasted that same sand?

*The voice of intelligence . . . is drowned by the roar of fear. It is ignored by the voice of desire. It is contradicted by the voice of shame. It is biased by hate and extinguished by anger. Most of all, it is silenced by ignorance.*

—DR. KARL MENNINGER

# THREE

# GHOSTS INSIDE

I FIRST MET Staff Sergeant Connel shortly after the terrorist attacks in New York. He was a good-looking kid who girls thought looked like Ethan Hawke. He was a few years younger than I was, and he had an obnoxious way of turning up his lip whenever he was thinking of something particularly nasty to do.

Connel had been part of the Tenth Mountain Division before the war, and since I was previously with the 101st Airborne, there was naturally some lighthearted rivalry. It began as meaningless banter that took place between all of us prior-service guys, but Connel became notorious for taking it over the top, making it personal. Within a few months of beginning our train-up for war, he was the bane of everyone in our squad.

The problem was that Connel knew his shit. There was never any doubt about his technical or tactical knowledge. He could quote directly from the seven dash eight—the infantry equivalent of the Bible. Connel had a knack for combining his expansive tactical knowledge with superb ass-kissing skills. He was one of the youngest guys in the squad and he was fast-tracking, and we all knew it.

Promotions come fast in wartime to those who are in the proverbial right place and time. That was what Connel was looking for: glory, awards, and a place in history. Hell, we all wanted a little of that, but what most of us wanted more was to avoid spilling our guts in Iraq, guts that he seemed to care very little for.

From the first few days in Kuwait, I could tell that some-thing would eventually break. We were pulling guard ten hours at a time and then getting ten hours "off." Our off time included meals and countless odd jobs—details that had to be taken care of—so in reality we only got a few hours' sleep on this constant rotation. Sitting still in the frigid early-morning hours of the Kuwaiti winter on guard duty was pure torture, and it was impossible not to feel animosity toward the man who was curled up warmly in his bivy sack. Connel didn't pull guard; he believed his position as squad leader warranted him a certain amount of comfort.

We were shorthanded, soldiers went from one shift straight into the other, and we were all extremely aware that the other squad leaders were sitting at positions, giving their soldiers breaks. Throughout the entire time we worked together, he pulled guard only once, and that was the night of the invasion because he couldn't sleep. When he came to my position to shoot the shit, I threw him on the roster and told Pearson to sleep.

The problems were apparent, but it takes a lot more than some grumbling specialists and buck sergeants to relieve a squad leader. We turned instead to mockery and plotting. We looked for scorpions to put in his boots at night, but whenever we found one, we could never go through with it. There was an inability to disregard our responsibilities that held us back. At some level, we felt like we were all in the same shitty situation and everyone had to deal with it. His way of doing that just turned out to be a lot of bullshit and an arrogant streak a mile fucking wide. But as it turned out, the old saying "We often give our enemies the means with which to defeat us" came true, and that's where I will pick up.


DURING THE BLISTERING SUMMER of Baghdad, Alpha Company was tasked out with an additional duty. In the western edge of our sector was the old Ministry of Labor. It was a gutted six-story office building that recalled George Orwell's *1984*. The darkened offices and hallway were cluttered with all kinds of paperwork spilling out of pregnant file cabinets. Family photographs torn from the walls by looters lay on the ground like discarded baseball cards. Anything worth anything had been stolen, and what wasn't had been destroyed for childish pleasure.

In the lot adjacent to the MOL was an old chemical plant that was suspected in the much-vaunted hunt for weapons of mass destruction. When the unit that had been there pulled out, we had to provide a presence to keep a semblance of order and of course safeguard the stockpiles of sarin gas that we were sure were buried just beneath the surface.

I'm not sure that there was any real priority to the chemical plant, as I never heard of any inspectors visiting the site, but occasionally the news cameras and visiting politicians would stop by to get footage of Iraq's abandoned chemical machinery.

Important as our presence was, one thing is true about war: There is always more work than there are soldiers. Only two squads at a time were sent to the MOL. For one week, those eighteen soldiers would live in absolute squalor. Soldiers in combat can be remarkably disgusting, and the fact that we all at one time or another had minor bouts of dysentery didn't help. The building was full of rotting feces. Piles of it, along with MRE toilet paper, littered the floor. The heat had turned the building into an oven, and the smell was overpowering.

At any one time we had four soldiers on the roof, three at the front gate, and a few as roving guards. Meanwhile, one squad of nine men would sleep. This left the gargantuan building nearly unguarded. There were doors on every corner, and the roof guards, try as they might, couldn't watch every possible avenue of approach.

Not that anyone was trying to get into the building, but because we were so far from the nearest Coalition soldiers, that particular corner of the sector was very active. The sounds of war were so ever-present, they became a kind of silence. But there were constant fireworks displays of tracers. Flashes of light from explosions outdoors would rattle the windows and cast an eerie pallor onto our drawn faces as we smoked final cigarettes and lay down to rack for a few hours. We called it The Wild West. It was scary. The city seethed directly outside the walls of our little citadel, and we were desperately out-numbered.

Bunking next to me in an old lobby were Pearson and Farmer. We huddled together in the blackness and spoke in whispered voices. Eventually, we would discover the neigh-borhood pharmacies and their sleeping pills. As it was, we had nothing to help us block out the war outside. Pearson was a very quiet and introspective person most of the time. When-ever he was drunk, he would pull his boonie cap down over his eyes, stand on his bunk, and do his best rapper impression, but now he was subdued, speaking only when asked a direct ques-tion. His 203 grenade launcher lay next to him, and through the gloom I could make out the movement of him wiping sweat from his brow and looking around nervously.

Farmer, on the other hand, was a born talker. His easy smile belied the fact that he always seemed to be angry at someone, sure that he was being mistreated because of his race. He was a big guy with a good sense of humor, and because we usually got along, I often got tasked out to go have a talk with him be-cause someone felt he was being antisocial or uncooperative. Connel had tried all year to "break him," but one thing you could say for Farmer—he wasn't breaking for anyone. Built like an ox, he could carry all the weight you gave him and do

PT for days. While I could still work with my squad leader, Farmer and he definitely had a hate-hate relationship and couldn't even sit in the same room together. Farmer lay on his side facing me, his rifle cradled in his arms, his head resting on a makeshift pillow of gear. He stared out in the dark and chewed on a twig.

I broke the silence with a question aimed at only darkness: "What's up with your girl, man?"

"Fuck, dog, I don't know. Bitch been all weird in her letters; I think she got another man or some shit. Fucking bitch. What about you?"

"Fuck, I picked a girl who can't read or some shit. I don't get letters anymore." Farmer tried for a few seconds not to laugh, but the situation was too fucked up to fight it off.

It was basically the same conversation we always had, so soon enough the talking died down and we all lay there, succumbing to the paralyzing blackness. Every few minutes, we would get a glimpse of our surroundings whenever a flare or explosion came particularly close and pierced the gloom.

There was a strong wind that night, and as it whistled through the hallways, doors would slam open and shut and windows would screech open, jolting soldiers awake. It wasn't long before the three of us were sitting up again, certain that someone or something was in the building. At least three times I got up, grabbed my weapon and night-vision, and walked down the hallway, peering into empty rooms after some particularly eerie noise. I wasn't sure if I was looking for Iraqis or ghosts, but I was pretty sure the appropriate response was the same. My M-249 squad automatic weapon fired 850 rounds a minute, and if that didn't stop whatever was after me, then I had a problem that nothing would solve.

By two in the morning, we were trapped in the daze that comes when you're trying to sleep but are awoken every ten minutes. The silence between us was broken when a window crashed open in our room and a metallic clinking rolled through the room.

"Grenade!" one of us yelled, and I dove out the door I was lying next to. Pearson had a chance to roll a few times away from the sound and ended up in a corner, covering his head. Farmer just sort of let out a squeak and accepted his fate. He was too far away from cover for action to do any good. I lay prone outside the room, aware that none of my friends had made it out.

Silence followed. I waited for an explosion, but none came. Then: "Man, fuck this place! This is bullshit!" Confused, I crept back in and found Farmer leaning over a Coke can, shaking his head. A gust of wind had blown a window open and knocked the can off and onto the tile floor. Pearson spoke up, still not sure whether he should venture out from his corner.

"Crawford, this place is fucking haunted! I can't sleep here."

"You ain't gotta tell me twice. For once I agree. Let's get the fuck out of here." With my consensus, it was unanimous. We would go downstairs and sleep with First Squad, even though that meant automatic and unrelenting ridicule.

"Crawford, I thought you guys were sleeping upstairs,"

Sergeant Washington called out as we plodded into the room. I was draped in my gear, my poncho liner dragging behind me like a tired dog's tail.

"Yeah, but we thought we'd come down here for a while." Wash was one of the best soldiers I knew, and it seemed like the guy never slept or got beat down by a situation like the rest of us.

"You fuckers aren't scared, are you?" Gleason chimed in. An amateur bodybuilder, Gleason was a monster of a man who I once saw punch a car to stop it in its tracks. The scary thing was that the dent his fist caused crumpled the air filter and the car actually did putter to a halt.

"Fuck you, man, it's haunted up there," I said with a laugh, hoping the taunting would pass, but of course it didn't.

"Well, shit, come on down here and let First Squad protect you. Do you want to lie down next to me and spoon? I can hold you if you like, sweetie," Sergeant Sims crooned from the corner.

Even Gaddis got in on it with his slow, methodical voice. "Fucking pussies," he drawled without rolling over or even looking at us. There was no escape from it, so we just smiled and nodded our heads while we found places to lie down.

I sat next to Wash for a while to shoot the shit, and when it was his turn to go to the front gate for guard, I joined him. "Shit, man, don't look like I'll be sleeping anyway." He was happy for the company. When you work with the same eight people day in and day out for months, it's a relief to talk to someone different. The sun was already bleaching the horizon by that time, and I found myself in the little two-room shack next to a torn-up fence saddled by concertina wire with Washington and Specialist Ramirez.

I'd known Ramirez for a few years too, but we weren't close. We had different cliques, and though we were both cordial and he seemed like a good enough soldier, we'd had some confrontations with each other in the past. The three of us sat there looking out at the four-lane highway. The constant parade of junked-out cars failed to entertain us as it once had. Trunks and doors hung precariously from rusty hinges, and every third car was a Volkswagen Passat, which we had once found unaccountably hilarious. We took turns, two of us sitting inside the building sipping on Arabic Pepsi, the third person lying behind the M-240 machine gun we had placed on the roof of the shack. There was no shade up there, and after an hour, your uniform would be as soaked as if you had sat through a monsoon.

It was still fairly early in the day when the radio crackled to life and I heard Staff Sergeant Connel's voice break through the static.

"Raptor Three-one, this is Raptor Three-two, over."

"Three-two, this is Three-one Bravo, go ahead, over."

"Three-one Bravo, go ahead and wake up Three-two Bravo and two other guys ASAP, over."

"Roger that, over."

"Three-two out." The radio went silent again, and I looked over at Washington confused. "Where has Connel been all morning?"

"All I was told is that he went with y'all's Alpha Team to go get some food."

"Does Raptor Main know they're out there?"

"Don't know, man," Wash answered, sounding like he couldn't be less interested. It was hot and he wasn't in much of a mood to talk, so I double-timed it back to the building to wake up Sergeant Kreed Howell. We all just called him Kreed, much to the chagrin of Connel, who could order us around but couldn't get an ounce of camaraderie or respect.

"Kreed, wake up. Connel wants us to haul ass out to the gate. He needs us for a patrol or something fucking pronto." I didn't have to tell Kreed twice. He was just as tired as the rest of us of Connel's constant bitching, and it was best just to follow his instructions to the letter than to hear him complain.

"All right man, sounds good. I'll be down in a sec," Kreed answered groggily, shaking off the sleep, and with a minimum amount of cursing, he rolled over and threw on his body armor.

I ran back to the gate and asked Washington if Connel had called in since I had been gone.

"Naw, man, not a peep." Even as I wondered what the hurry could be, a Humvee came racing in the gate and squealed to a halt next to us, Connel and an interpreter inside.

"Get in, Crawford! Where the fuck is Howell?" Connel growled.

"He's on his way, Sar'nt," I answered as I crawled into the backseat of the gunship. It's always a tight fit with body armor and weapon, and it becomes easiest just to ride with one foot out of the vehicle sort of half in, half out. We didn't wear seat belts, and the doors had long since been taken off so that we could jump out of a burning vehicle if need be. Even as I got comfortable, Kreed came up huffing and puffing, but it wasn't fast enough for Connel.

"Goddamnit! I said ASAP! You gotta move when I tell you to move!"

"Roger, Sar'nt" was his mumbled response, but he didn't even look up when he said it. Ramirez jumped in opposite me, his relief having already taken his place on the gun. Off we went into the smog-filled Iraqi street, weaving in and out of traffic like an ambulance. Unable to contain my curiosity, I leaned forward.

"Hey, Sar'nt, where we going? What's the deal?" Surprisingly, Connel turned to face me and was actually smiling.

"Man, we hit a house this morning. Brunelle and Whittaker are still there. The place is full of weapons and money! No fucking shit, man!"

Kreed looked at Connel with an open mouth. Brunelle and Whittaker were alone in the city somewhere and had just been left.

"What house?" he asked. There was a nervous anticipation, the kind of sick feeling I imagine you get on a plane that's crashing and there isn't anything to do but ride it in. Connel was on a roll, though, and didn't notice our wariness.

"Some hajji came in with a tip last night when I was at the gate. Said there were fedayeen terrorists in this house down the road. We went to check it out this morning and were compromised by the owner, so we just took it. It's right up here past this light to the left." He sounded like a kid who has just gotten a brand-new ten-speed bike.

In the eyes of the battalion commander, the edge of our

sector may as well have been the ends of the earth. To them, if you went too far you just fell into a never-ending chasm of darkness. We were already a mile or two past that point now, and despite being afraid that I already knew the answer, I dared one more question.

"Sar'nt, isn't that pretty far out of sector? How did you get Raptor Main to okay that?" I had no problem going out of sector to roll up some hajjis, but I liked to know that the omnipotent power of the United States Army had my back.

"I didn't tell them. Dude, you gotta see this shit. There's like a million dollars in there."

The trepidation was giving way to excitement. Everyone wanted to make a big bust, be heroes of the day. We would get awards, maybe even make the news. Somewhere in the back of my mind, an angry voice chided me. Pearson and Farmer were still at the MOL asleep. The interpreter eyed us nervously. Our squad minus a few was going alone into enemy-occupied territory in a soft-bodied Humvee. What's worse is that no one in the world except hajji knew we were coming.

We cruised down a couple of lonely alleyways full of the rubble of torn-down buildings. Great piles of trash ten feet high littered the corners. The stench from rotting food was compounded by the fact that all the clutter had clogged up the drainage system coming from inside the nearby shanties. Streams and lakes of sewage crisscrossed the streets and lots. Groups of local children frolicked about in them. Their cheering at our approach turned to rock-throwing jeers when we passed them by.

"Lovely people," Ramirez noted as we drove. I didn't need

to answer. I just watched out my open door, one leg hanging out brushing inches above the ground, the muzzle of my weapon protruding out the side of our vehicle like a cannon.

We came to a stop next to a high mud-brick wall that engulfed a fairly modern house. Connel immediately dismounted.

"Kreed, you and Harris stay with the fifty. Crawford, Ramirez, c'mon," Connel yelled back at us, already five or six bounds into the iron gate, which hung open like a gaping mouth. Ramirez and I broke into a jog to catch up. In the driveway was a shit-brown BMW, and I passed it with a sideways glance. "Who picked that fucking color? Fucking hajjis got no fucking taste," Ramirez commented, and I smiled. My desert boots trampled the flowers in their well-manicured lawn, something that gave me rare pleasure.

"Friendlies coming in!" Connel yelled as he reached the door and opened it. I followed closely behind him and was immediately impressed. The house wasn't lavish by American standards, but it was certainly upper class. There was thousands of dollars of audio and video equipment nestled in between leather couches and an antique wooden dining table. A glass chandelier swung from the ceiling. On the floor of the living room sat two dirty Iraqis with their hands flexicuffed behind their backs. One was young, maybe sixteen at most, and the other looked to be in his late twenties. Whittaker stood behind them, his rifle trained absentmindedly on their backs.

"Look what we found," he said with a smile.

"Yeah, man, I see," I answered, still taking the room in. An amiable voice came from the back of the house.

"Crawford, is that you? Come here, man, you gotta see this shit." It was Brunelle, and I scrambled past an overturned desk into a back bedroom, Connel close behind me.

"Holy shit." The room was utterly trashed, clothes strewn about and boxes dumped out. It was nicer than most Iraqi bedrooms, mostly because there was actually a bed in it instead of just a thin mattress and a pile of rags on the floor. On the bed, arranged concentrically, were five AK-47 rifles, a revolver, and three large rice bags full of money—two with dinars, the third with American dollars. The exchange rate at that time was around fifteen hundred dinars to one dollar, but there was easily a few hundred thousand worth of crisp, sweet-smelling American bucks. Connel, Brunelle, and I took turns posing on the bed, money in our laps and all around us. We must've looked like the bank robbers from the gangland days of America, except instead of tommy guns we held AK-47s in either hand.

"Did you guys check upstairs yet?" I asked, caught up in the moment and eager to find my own loot.

"Not really. I mean, we cleared it, but that's about it. Go see what you can find." Brunelle's smile was ear to ear, and without answering I wheeled and trotted up the stairs, weapon still at the ready. The furnishings were much more spartan upstairs. In fact, there was no furniture at all to speak of. One whole room was full of the wooden boxes that rifles are shipped in. I checked a few and they seemed to all be empty. In one corner was a pile of computer equipment, complete with manuals on the Apache helicopter and M-1 Abrams tank.

Against a wall, a missile-guidance system was sitting right on the floor.

At the far side of the room was a door. I was sure it opened onto the roof. Most of the houses there are built that way so that during the hot summer months residents can sleep in the open air for a bit of respite. I was startled to hear a noise on the other side of it, and with wariness I crept next to it. After a deep breath, I kicked it open and came through, weapon on my shoulder, safety off. There was a shadow moving quickly behind a corner.

"Come out, motherfucker!" I yelled, instantly aware that the chances anyone spoke English were slim to none. But apparently I was being clear enough: The shadow moved closer, and around the corner peered the curious nose of a German shepherd puppy. It panted in the sweltering sun. Laughing, I lowered my weapon.

"Hey, Buddy, whatcha doin'?" I clucked, going down on one knee for licks to my hand and face. The dog was more than happy to accommodate me, and his frantic wiggling brought a smile to my tired face. At least someone in Iraq was happy to see me.

When I went back downstairs empty-handed, Buddy came bounding behind me. Brunelle was at the foot of the stairs, looking at something in his grimy hand. "Hey, man, take a look at this shit." He handed me a couple of Polaroids; no more smiles for me.

"Fuck, man, these are some bad fucking dudes." The pictures were of a man being tortured. A man sat in the center of a room with a black bag over his head. Two men stood over him like hunters on a weekend hunting trip to Alabama.

We stood in silence for a moment, and then Connel pounced on the POWs. "Fedayeen motherfucker? You know what the fuck I'm saying!" He was up in one kid's face while the other looked on fearfully. Neither said anything. "Whose car is that out front? Ask him!" Connel motioned to the interpreter, then to one of the kneeling prisoners. The interpreter, a thin man in his mid-thirties, stroked his mustache nervously and then began speaking. The bad thing about interpreters is they think of themselves as the negotiators, and they always end up having ten-minute conversations with someone over a simple question like "Whose car is that?"

After it became apparent that neither of the people on the floor was claiming the brown BMW, Connel motioned to Ramirez and Brunelle and the three went outside to search it. I took my place with Whittaker, lazily watching our prisoners. After a few minutes of muddled conversation outside, I heard the crashing of a car window. This elicited a groan from one of the prisoners. I laughed.

"Your car after all, huh? Well, joke's on you, motherfucker." I leaned against a wall and watched as Buddy chewed on someone's rubber sandal under the stairwell.

More commotion outside, and I stepped to the window and parted the curtain. Regardless of the semblance of control we had, we were still six Americans alone in Baghdad, and the yelling in the driveway reminded me of our tenuous hold on the situation. Connel opened the door with a smile.

"You're not gonna fucking believe this, man," he said to me with that upturned lip of his. Next to him, Brunelle and Ramirez ushered in three new POWs they had managed to collect, apparently without much effort.

"This motherfucker lives here—came right up and told us. This is his cousin and mother. They don't want us in their house." The last part was full of sarcasm. It was like a drug dealer walking over to the DEA agents raiding his house and asking them politely to leave.

"Criminals in Iraq are fucking stupid," Ramirez chimed in from the back.

"Fuck, the whole country is stupid," someone corrected. I took the two male prisoners we had just taken by the arm and dragged them into a second room. They had already been searched outside, so I just pushed them down on the floor. This space was much sparser than the bedroom in the back. It had a typical Iraqi bed on the floor—simply stated, a blanket and pillow. Once they were lying down, I flexicuffed them both and left Ramirez to watch them.

The mother, who appeared to be in her sixties, was ranting, raving, and spitting on us. I took her by the arm to the dining room table and instructed her to sit down. She struggled briefly, but the interpreter managed to let her know that we meant business, and with a final glare at all of us for dramatic effect, she sat down. Her beratings didn't cease, though, and even when we threw the pictures of her son torturing people at her she just shrugged her shoulders and continued her tirade. We had the interpreter tell her that we would gag her if she didn't stop talking, and after that she leaned back and was content with sending evil looks our way.

"Hey, check this out!" Connel yelled. He was again in the money room and had noticed some recent remodeling work on the wall. He had kicked in the weak spot, and in the divider between the walls were three more bags of cash. "Man, these guys really are fucking dirty. I mean, who the fuck hides money in their walls?" Meanwhile, Buddy was still prancing about, chewing on the shoe he had discovered. The old lady swung a poorly aimed kick at him, and he ran into the kitchen. I followed him in, figuring that he was probably hungry; the poor thing had all its ribs showing.

Everything was going great despite my earlier concerns. Connel stood calmly with Ramirez. Brunelle was with the two latecoming POWs in the other room, and Whittaker had gone outside to keep Kreed company. I was in the kitchen, fridge open, dumping all the edible food into a pot and feeding a more-than-eager Buddy.

When I went back into the living room, everything went to shit. Connel had pulled a wallet from one of the older prisoners and was looking for identification. It contained a military ID, and it was clear that the prisoner had previously been a soldier of some importance in the Iraqi army. There were pictures of him in grandeur, with his uniform on, all over the house. Inside the wallet was three hundred dollars. Connel held it out to me.

"What?" I asked. He gestured toward me with the money once more. "I don't fucking want it," I answered, maybe too fast. There was that upturned lip, that sneer that made me want to pounce on him.

"Fuck, man, don't say it—they might speak English. Ramirez, come here! And bring your camelback!" Ramirez sauntered in with his camelback riding low, like a tenth-grader who didn't bring any books to school anyway.

"Turn around." Ramirez did as he was told, with a quick glance at me for help. Seeing none, he allowed his camelback to be unzipped and loaded with cameras, radios, and other electronic equipment. Someone carried a boom box out to the Humvee. I looked around and saw the interpreter fingering a new nine-millimeter pistol before tucking it away in his belt. I hadn't counted the money before, but it was obvious there was no use now.

Pictures were being ripped from their frames and placed in pockets. Virtually anything small enough was carried out. It was ridiculous. None of the objects taken was worth anything. The electronics were all shitty, and what use is a few hundred dollars. Offer me a few hundred thousand and I'll be tempted. A couple hundred bucks is pocket change, and there wasn't shit in that country worth buying.

I felt ashamed when I saw how unsurprised the prisoners were. They had expected this all along, whether from lack of respect for us or because they were accustomed to this treatment from the old Saddam regime. They always seemed to have a fatalistic viewpoint. Allah willed Saddam to fall, just as he would when America fell. They just accepted the abuse in the meantime as part of life. I shook my head, thinking how

disappointed my mom would have been if she could have seen
this. When I called home, she always ended the conversation
by telling me in her nasal Boston accent, "Johnny, remember
you're a Christian boy." It was the one and only time during
the war that I was embarrassed by our behavior. We had looted
in Nasiriyah, but that was during the invasion, and all the previous occupants were dead. With a silent grunt, I walked out
the door.

When I was back in the noon sun, the sweat began running
anew. I staggered as if under a burden out to the Humvee,
where a slight crowd had formed. Kreed, Whittaker, and Harris were looking very ready to leave as they eyed the passersby
stopping for a closer look. I exchanged a few words with them
and then heard the radio squawk.

"Raptor Three-two, this is Raptor Six, over."

"Three-two, this is Six, what is your situation? Over." It was
the company commander, trying to find out where we were
and what the fuck was up with us. I looked at Kreed, who
shook his head, and then I called Connel on the squad radio.
He was right inside, but I wasn't going back in there now.

"Wu-Tang [Connel's handle], this is Porn Star. The Raptor
Six element wants a sitrep. Over."

"Roger, Porn Star. Go ahead and give them our grid. Don't
tell them details, just a grid, and tell them we need a vehicle to
move this shit. Over."

I leaned into the Humvee and grabbed the hand mike. I
wasn't eager to have anything more to do with this operation,
but if there was one person I hated more than Connel, it was
our company commander.

"Raptor Six, this is Raptor Three-two, over."

"Go ahead, Three-two."

"Sitrep follows. Over."

"Go ahead, Three-two. Over." There was anticipation or angst in the commander's voice, and I wasn't sure which I disliked more.

"Be advised, we have five enemy prisoners. Break. We have four rifles, one pistol, and a large amount of money. Also a lot of PIR here, break." PIR was the intelligence we were always looking for, the things that the military intelligence would want to look at: the computers, missile-guidance system, and so on.

"Three-two actual requests addition personnel and also a five-ton truck to move the PIR, over."

"That's a good copy, Three-two. What's your grid? Over." I sent our location and then tossed the hand mike back onto the passenger seat of our Humvee.

I swallowed my pride and walked back into the house, rolling my eyes at Kreed as I passed. He chuckled, knowing my disdain for Connel and his hasty plans.

"Hey, Sar'nt, Six element is sending a five-ton truck and personnel to help secure the area and move all this shit." Connel didn't even look up at me, and I knew I was on his shit list for not taking the money earlier. If everyone took part, then we could all lie together. That was why he had sent Whittaker outside and why he had left Farmer and Pearson behind: Connel had left in the house only people that he assumed would be in on it. I had talked often enough about how much I'd like to have seen the Saddam millions, and he must have assumed I would be down. Without a word from him, I walked away and into the room where Brunelle was holding the original prisoners. I told him I'd take over for him.

I sat in a chair against the wall and rested my machine gun on my lap, facing the barrel in the general direction of the two prisoners who were prostrated on the ground.

"So what's up, guys?" I asked the prisoners. Just because someone doesn't speak the same language doesn't mean a bored soldier won't make conversation. I once heard Mitchell carry on a twenty-minute conversation about *The Little Mermaid* with a very confused prisoner. So I went ahead and told them I liked their living room design but felt that the bags of money in the wall were a little excessive. I asked when the last time they tortured someone was and told them I liked their dog. We talked about sports and politics. Occasionally, they would answer with the generic responses all our prisoners used: "Mister, baby, hospital." It was the same old line that everyone tried on us.

"Oh, your baby is in the hospital. Man, that sucks. Anyway, so like I was saying . . ." and I continued in the same manner. It wasn't that we were particularly nasty to our prisoners; we just didn't really care about their final destination. It wasn't our concern, nor were the politics involved. The worst I ever saw a prisoner treated was down in our little POW collection point: A man sat in the corner like a scolded child. The sand-bag on his head had a frown drawn on it, and above him was a sign that read, "I am in time-out because I have a potty mouth."

When my conversation with the two prisoners was drawing to a close, I began to hear new American voices in the front yard and in came a stream of soldiers. Our company commander led the way. His nine-millimeter Beretta waved back and forth in his hand like John Fucking Wayne. There was no use telling him the building was already secure. Without a pistol in his hand, he wouldn't have looked like a conqueror. The CO leaned into the room, looked absentmindedly around as if taking it all in.

"Hey there, got this under control, soldier?" He patted me on the back and gave me some kind of faux fatherly smile.

"Roger that, sir," I replied with a genuine fuck-you smile. We'd been together almost a year and the son of a bitch still didn't know most of our names.

"Good, good, you boys did great today." And with that he was out, no doubt preparing his victory speech. Other soldiers filed in. Boner, Kerr, and all of Third Squad had brought vehicles to tote out everything we were confiscating. They passed bags of money and weapons by the armful out to the waiting vehicles. With a yell, the time had come to leave, and I grabbed my two prisoners by the arm, hauling them to their feet, and followed them out the door. While they along with all the loot went back to our main compound, the six of us loaded up and headed back to the MOL.

The sun was low on the horizon and shadows stretched their fingers out to reach us as we pulled into our little haunted home away from home. I was too tired to field many questions from Farmer and Pearson, and when darkness fell so did I, exhausted. Fuck the ghosts. I was asleep almost at once, and slept unusually well.

Third Squad showed up to relieve us as the first glint of sunlight came over the dust-covered shanties and rundown apartment buildings. They weren't supposed to be there for al-most a week, so it was quite a surprise.

"What's going on, Sar'nt?" I asked Sellers.

"Dude, there are fucking reporters and everything back there. They want to interview you guys. And the colonel is supposed to talk to you guys too. Fucking 'heroes of the war' and shit."

"No shit?" I laughed incredulously. We both knew that people did more heroic things getting out of bed in the morn-ing, but we had added a big plus sign to both our company and battalion commanders' officer evaluation reports, and for that we were heroic enough to them.

"Yeah, we're here so you guys can go back and be all pho-togenic and shit."

It didn't take long to get my squad ready to go, and on the ride back we were buzzing. I spent the ride talking with Brunelle, theorizing about what we would say to the blond newswoman from Fox or the brunette from CNN. They were some beautiful newscasters, and every time they came near us, we would stare longingly at them. We jokingly practiced pin-ning medals on our chests. We would have to call home to tell our families what time to watch the news.

The gate flew open upon our arrival, but there was no ticker-tape parade, and if there were any reporters there, I didn't see them. The only thing that awaited us was our loom-ing bear of a platoon sergeant. He stood with his arms crossed across his massive chest, glowering at us as we unloaded off the Humvee.

"Go on up and wait in your room. I'll come get you guys

later," he growled. He looked us all up and down, groaned audibly, shook his head, and walked away, his broad back casting an enormous shadow on the ground as he moved.

"Oh shit," Kreed whispered in my ear. The earlier rosiness of our cheeks was now a nervous pallor.

For the rest of the day, we sat quietly in our room wondering what was going on. No one dared venture downstairs to get a candy bar or Coke from the company store. I read a book, Kreed listened to his headphones, Connel cleaned his rifle, but none of us could concentrate. There was only one thought on our minds: The army had very visibly taken a hard stance on looting, and the news had already been full of reports of soldiers who were arrested for the very same things we had done the previous day.

Brunelle, Kreed, and Connel—the noncommissioned officers of our squad—were called downstairs first. They stood before a very irate commander and filled out witness statements after much ass-chewing, I'm sure. For Kreed and Brunelle it should have been a cakewalk; neither one was in the room when anything bad happened. Connel, on the other hand, was in a predicament. He was present throughout, and not only did he fail in his responsibility as squad leader to put a stop to things, he actually instigated it.

Before long, someone came up and fetched Ramirez to go down. When he came back a few hours later, his head was down and he had a forlorn look in his eyes.

"What's going on, man? What did they say?" I asked him as he wearily overcame the last step to our floor. I assumed they'd be coming for me next.

"Dude, I'm in deep shit. They know I took all that shit from the house. I'm getting fucking fried." His voice was defeated; I had never been particularly tight with him, but fuck.

"Well, I was there, and Connel was the one who put all that shit in your assault pack. I mean, it was an unlawful order, but it's his responsibility—he's the squad leader."

"Crawford, it's more complicated than that. That wasn't the platoon sergeant asking questions, it was the fucking CIA." Ramirez was right. I knew how things worked in the army and in our unit. Connel at the worst was gonna get a slap on the wrist, and this poor college kid was getting fucked big time.

"Dude, this shit should be on Connel" was all I could offer.

"I don't know, man. I think I'm just gonna take this one." With that, Ramirez turned slothlike and headed toward his cot. I didn't really know the extent of the thievery, nor did I know what the punishments were, but it seemed like he was on his way to Fort Leavenworth. I knew someone who got sent there once, and he said it was the worst place in the world. It's all the fun times of the army combined with the joy of federal pound-me-in-the-ass prison.

Connel, of course, had been no slouch, and assuming something bad might happen, he had hid all the loot back at the MOL before we were ever picked up. That night Sergeant Golder and some unwilling volunteers went back to The Wild West to get the evidence. Kreed and I ended up going along as security. I drove, and he sat next to me in the passenger seat. As we swerved down the empty streets, we yelled over the wind roaring in our ears. The gunner was behind and above us, so we had relative privacy.

"Dude, you know Ramirez is taking the fall for all that

shit?" I bitched aloud without taking my eyes off the swiftly moving road.

"Well, he took the shit, right?" Kreed was as tired as I was of the whole deal.

"Yeah, he took it, but fucking Connel put the shit in his assault pack. I mean, shit, just 'cause he didn't carry it out on his back, he still had just as big a part in stealing it—more, actually, since he was in charge."

Kreed was quiet for a few seconds, and then he answered. "Well, you saw the whole thing—why don't you say something?"

"What the fuck can I say? He's my fucking squad leader. I can't really sell him out."

Kreed was silent, and I wished I had put that fucking scorpion in Connel's boot when I had the chance.

"It's their decision, I guess. I'm just glad I'm not part of it," I said into the wind. The rest of the ride was quiet. We pulled up to the MOL, and I left the engine running and sat behind the steering wheel in the uncomfortable seat, absentmindedly running my finger across my weapon. I didn't notice Golder walk up to me, but when he cleared his throat I came back to life.

"Kreed said you got something to tell me, Crawford." I had a hell of a lot of respect for the platoon sergeant, and I knew I couldn't lie to him—he'd see right through me, and he probably already did. I got out of the Humvee and walked with him, away from the building about thirty meters into the darkened shadows beneath a fig tree. Beams of moonlight cast leopard spots of light on the ground beneath my feet.

I looked at Sergeant Golder and then quickly dropped my eyes to the ground. Shit, I felt like a thirteen-year-old kid explaining a bad report card.

"What's the deal with Ramirez? What are they gonna do to him once all this is over?" Golder stared at me. I couldn't see it in the darkness, but I could feel his eyes burrowing into my soul.

"I don't know for sure. The commander wants to push it all the way to make an example. Remember those guys from Bravo Company that got in trouble for stealing all that shit a few months ago? Well, they all lost their rank—there were a bunch of them, and this is all on one guy. I don't know how bad it'll be for him, but it ain't gonna be pleasant."

Sergeant Golder paused long enough to spit some Copenhagen out of his engorged lip, and I could hear it splash onto the dry ground. I nervously shifted my weight from one foot to the other, and my hands fidgeted on my machine gun. Every so often I would look up, only to find him still eyeing me. Golder had a fatherly way about him, and I hated to think we had all disappointed him that bad.

"Sar'nt, I don't want to narc on anyone—that shit ain't right."

"Crawford, you know the difference between right and wrong. If you have something to tell me, now is the time." He never raised his voice, but there was a force in it that struck me like a blow and my mind reeled. The battle was over and he had prevailed. I took a breath and then told Golder what had happened. As I spoke, I could see waves of anger flashing behind his eyes. With a sigh, I finished and felt my body slump. I felt like the biggest piece of shit ever.

He just clapped me on the shoulder with his bear paw of a hand and turned back toward the vehicle. Six feet later, his mammoth frame stopped and he glanced back. "You did the right thing, Crawford." Then he left me alone with my guilt.

The next few days were nothing if not awkward. The company was full of rumors about what had gone down. Ramirez got a summarized Article 15—a slap on the wrist, really—and the rest of us were off scot-free. Connel was relieved of his position, and pending punishment, he was restricted to quarters. While Kreed led patrols as our temporary squad leader, Connel would sit in our room and read Whittaker's Bible with the religious fervor of a guilty man. Soon thereafter, he was busted down one rank to buck sergeant and sent to another platoon. At his request, he was moved over to Staff Sergeant McGuinn's squad. McGuinn was a hard man from Ranger Battalion who didn't take shit from anyone other than his girlfriend. Connel didn't exactly mesh there, and within a month he had developed a mysterious chest condition that precluded the wearing of body armor. He was put on permanent profile and spent the rest of the war monitoring the radio from the command post. Although he never confronted me, I'm sure he was aware that I was the only one who could have told the truth. We passed each other every day but never spoke again.

Kreed was promoted to staff sergeant, and life in Second Squad improved drastically. We almost began to have a good time.

Months later, when we returned to the States in February, soldiers were met by friends and family members. I stood in formation inside of a gym looking for a familiar face, when I saw a sign. It read "Welcome Home Staff Sergeant Connel" and was held by a proud mother. My cheeks blushed with shame; I had done the right thing for the wrong reasons. I would have lied my ass off for a friend, but Connel and I had never been friends. I had wanted him gone and had gotten my wish, and now there was no way I could ever make it right again.

FOUR

# SOUTHERN BOYS

R APTOR SIX, this is Raptor Three-two. We have target vehicle in sight—it is traveling westbound on target road.
Can we take it? Over."

"Do you see any weapons yet, Three-two?"

"Negative, Six, but this will be the fourth pass in less than
an hour, and that's definitely the right vehicle. Over."

"Negative on the intercept, Three-two. We want to catch
them in the act. Do not take them yet."

Sergeant Howell threw down the hand mike

"Fucking idiot!" He spit as if to avert the growing distaste in
all our mouths.

"I swear to God, the old man won't be happy until he gets us killed." We were all contorted into odd positions on the concrete ground, hunting for comfort that wasn't there. The sun had long since set, but the heat was still oppressive and sweat rained down my back. It was close to eleven at night, and the tension had our nerves worn thin; we had set up our ambush at midday and had been waiting ever since.

Without looking up, Sergeant Brunelle flicked the glowing embers of his cigarette away.

"Naw, man, it's all right. We're hunting them."

"Fucking-A right! Fucking killer squad." Sellers lounged against a mud-brick wall, trying in earnest to spit tobacco onto an emaciated chicken scrounging through the courtyard.

The night before, a so far unnamed hajji had come to the gate asking to speak to our commander. He was instead directed to the intelligence officer, a career National Guardsman who was overweight and underintelligent. With thick, plastic-rimmed glasses crammed onto cellulose cheeks, he was an embarrassment to all of us, as were most of the officers in our battalion. Where we were students looking for a free education, they were career National Guardsmen. It is the downfall of the National Guard system: incompetent officers with neither the experience nor the drive to lead men in combat.

But the mission had so far gone off without a hitch. During the operations order, it was learned that the informant was a disgruntled fedayeen member who, like so many of the Iraqis in our sector, was more than willing to sell his neighbors out to the Coalition forces for personal gain. What this particular hajji had against his former comrades I didn't know, and didn't really care. He had given us everything we needed: a time, description, and mode of attack.

The idea was for three insurgents—two with rocket-propelled grenades and the third, our informant, as a getaway driver—to launch a harassing attack against our barracks. At the time, my battalion was living in the old Republican Guard officers' club. Until very recently a popular hangout of Uday and Qusay, it was littered with wet bars and private rooms where the two sons of America's second-greatest enemy would snatch schoolgirls off the street and assault them, often killing their families afterward if any complaints were made. At least this was the story the neighbors told us. True or not, their love for us was immediately related to the number of MREs we handed out to the hungry locals who congregated on the rooftops around our building. Before long, even onetime Coalition fans could be heard chanting, "With our blood, bodies, and souls we will free you, Saddam!"

We had been the subject of several attacks in the weeks prior, and the ear-rending explosions of rocket-propelled grenades slamming into our home had become commonplace. We were Americans, of this there was no doubt; most of us were from Florida, a few from Georgia, all Southern boys, some with roots tracing back to the last time the Florida militia was really called up, in what we jokingly referred to as the war of northern oppression. We had names like John, and Steven, and Terry. We didn't eat dried lamb's heads or pay any heed to the five-times-daily call to prayer, but things had changed. We might not have belonged, but it became our town, our block, our home, and we got to feeling that it wasn't right that some fucker could come in and blow up our house.

My platoon moved out just past midday, and by three everyone was in place. The informant drove his Chevrolet Malibu three times around the ambush site just so that we could all get a good look at it. The setting sun shone off of the rust-speckled blue paint. We all noted the bad brake light, the Jordanian license plate, and the missing back left hubcap.

Third Squad had set in with a sniper team at the old soccer stadium. Used shortly before the war as a staging area for an Iraqi airborne brigade, the field was littered in shit and maggots. They kept security on our rear in case anyone should try to outflank our position. The driver had told us that the plan involved him parking the car outside the stadium; then the two collaborators would move down what we had deemed "target road" with bags filled with rocket-propelled grenades. It was a short walk, but RPGs are notoriously ill at long-distance shots, and the two attackers planned to move to the southern edge of our compound and then volley-fire both their rockets over the wall and onto our heads. Then they would flee in their Chevy Malibu like outlaws on an old TV series.

In between them and five hundred sleeping soldiers sat the nine of us in Second Squad. We had holed up inside the courtyard of a friendly neighbor. The attack was supposed to occur at ten P.M. We had gotten in position so early so as to avoid any surveillance the enemy might set up close to attack time. We counted the minutes as they passed. Ten-foot-high concrete walls on either side lined the road the enemy would come down. Whenever our front man got a good look at the two men and their weapons, we would all surge forth like an angry storm, weapons blazing. Both men would have to be dead before they realized what was happening. If either managed to get a shot off at that range, with concrete surrounding us, a rocket was assured to find a target, and there would be no way to avoid heavy casualties from the shrapnel. There would be no second chances—not like when we shot the hajji in the nuts a few nights before, or when Gleason had taken a driver with a kidney shot. This had to be a "center of mass," overwhelming firepower attack. Sergeant Howell had placed Whigham and me toward the front. We were the squad automatic machine gunners. Our weapons fired upward of 850 bullets a minute, and could certainly lay down the amount of death that was necessary for the job. Still, one mistake and we had a mass-casualty situation on our hands.

We passed the time as best we could. Sergeant Howell sat next to Sergeant Golder and talked about working out, how to increase their bench presses and break the next plateau. Most of us spent a lot of time in our homemade gym. Some soldiers were making huge gains, but then steroids weren't illegal in Iraq, and are illegal in the army only on paper. As for drugs that make you stronger and more aggressive, the army could only pray we were all participating. Me, I was more of a Valium and Prozac type of guy, anything to chill me out, get me a buzz. Beer and whiskey were easy to get but hard to hide, and hangovers are not the way to spend a busy day in 130-degree heat.

Brunelle sat next to Whigham. They were an odd pair, always together. Whigham rarely if ever spoke, which was fine with Brunelle, who rarely if ever stopped talking. He rambled on about Ranger school, bike week, his brother, and especially girls, our favorite subject—what girls we had seduced in high school or college, each becoming more beautiful and loose with every telling. Since coming to Iraq, we had all received e-mails from lost loves or lusts, proclaiming how much they missed us, how they couldn't wait for our return. Those of us who were married brooded over lost opportunities whenever the single guys fantasized about the orgies they would return to back at college. As he talked, Brunelle would glance through the tiny crack we had left open in the compound's heavy iron gate.

Against the opposite wall, Pearson and Hightower sat alone together, an equally odd couple, so close that they had begun to behave like an old married couple. Pearson was so tall and evening black that the hajjis insisted he was from Sudan, at which he would smile with pearly white teeth and with a shake of his head say, "Naw, Panama City, man, Panama City." Hightower, a slight country boy from some lost town in the panhandle of Florida, was ever diligent in his shadowing of Pearson. I didn't like him—he was a complainer, and if I or Sergeant Sellers weren't constantly checking him, he would leave behind his heavier equipment. He would take out the ceramic plates from his Interceptor body armor and go virtually unprotected out on patrol. I don't know how he did it; I felt naked any time I took mine off, and I lived in constant anticipation of the sharp pain of an unseen sniper putting a bullet through my back.

Whittaker sat alone, leaning up against a wall in the shade, looking troubled. He had that nervous twitch that made his eyes blink every few moments and leave him looking confused. We'd had a few laughs at his expense. We all had nicknames, and his was Preacher. A devout Southern Baptist, he harped on us day and night about our sinful misguided ways. He was an outcast among us, unable to curse or talk about drinking and girls. On top of all that, we all had our doubts over whether or not he was a "trigger puller"—whether or not he could take a serious shot at someone—whereas the rest of us had come to live for the moment.

We had been trained. People pick the army—they become mechanics, water-supply specialists, cooks, clerks—but the infantry is different. The infantry picks the man: men who do poorly in math, excel at athletics, drink a lot, love their mothers, fear their fathers; men who have something to prove or feel they have already proven it all. We were both proud and ashamed of what we were. The stepchildren of the army, infantrymen are like guard dogs at a rich man's house. When people come to visit, the media, the USO, they lock us in the garage and tell us not to bark, but when night falls and there is a noise outside, everyone is glad we're there. And that's what we were out there doing that night, guarding against bumps in the night.

Sergeant Sellers was my team leader. He was vivacious and fun-loving one moment, seemed depressed and suicidal the next. We got along great. My only problem with him was that I often found myself stopping the rest of the team and setting them into security while I chased Sellers down some side alley where he was trying to catch a chicken or kick a can. He saw the whole world as a game, and maybe he was more right than the rest of us.

At the moment, Sellers was trying his best to impress the women of the house. The husband had come out into the courtyard only momentarily to shake our hands, perhaps nervous about our presence, more likely perturbed that there were nine sex-crazed killers in his yard. The mother, grandmother, and daughter all sat at a safe distance, absorbing our every move, mimicking us like children. Our interpreter, a decrepit man, sat with them, explaining the parts of our conversation they couldn't catch.

Sellers spent most of that evening in one corner with Sajeeda, the nineteen-year-old girl who lived there, trying like a schoolboy to impress her. At one point he walked to an empty propane tank and, feigning a great feat of strength, lifted it over his head with much groaning and straining. "See, I am very masculine, make many babies," he said, imitating the way the hajjis talked to us. The old grandmother pushed past him and lifted the same propane tank high into the air, her eighty-year-old frame taut with stress. We all laughed out loud at that, and then laughed even harder as Sellers's face grimaced in embarrassment.

Sajeeda ran inside to get DVDs to show us.

"American movies," she managed in broken English. She had *Rambo* and *Hot Shots*, but they had been edited. In the background of both covers was the image of Saddam Hussein, pistol in hand, preparing to execute the American infidels who starred in the films. We laughed, and even though there was a side room with a DVD player in it, no one took the opportunity to watch one.

"I don't fucking like it, man—why don't we just hit the car next time it passes. We go out in that street, man, gonna be messy. Send us home stamped 'Members Missing,'" Brunelle stated matter-of-factly.

Sergeant Golder, the platoon sergeant, shrugged his wide shoulders. What could he do? The company commander was running the show. Captain Sanchez was a former police officer from Tampa, and he wanted to do it the way cops do it: Wait till we see a weapon and then confront the perpetrators. Not a great plan when the weapons in question are two rocket-propelled grenades locked and loaded and coming at you, but what the hell, he was behind three or four walls inside a building, safe as a baby suckling his mother.

"Fuck, man, there it goes again." Whigham spoke up uncharacteristically. "That's five times, Sergeant, and all three dicks are inside. We can take these motherfuckers. Me and Crawford go out there and leave that car a smoking wreck, man, nothing but benzene and blood left when we're done." Sergeant Golder called it in to the CP.

"Raptor Six, this is Raptor Three-seven. We had the target vehicle pass by again, this time going west on target road, over." Before the commander could answer, our sniper observation post on the west building called in as well.

"Raptor Six this is OP Two, I confirm target vehicle just took a right onto route bravo and is now headed north. He's doing laps around the compound, over." Captain Sanchez, inside the command post, waited a few moments, undoubtedly reveling in the drama unfolding around him.

"Raptor Three-seven, this is Raptor Six. Do not—I say again, do not—intercept the vehicle until it stops and the two individuals dismount and prepare to attack. We don't want to hit the informant, over."

"Roger, Three-seven out." Sergeant Golder looked at us as if to say, "See, I told you so."

"Man, that motherfucker don't care about the informant, he just doesn't want a fuckup." It was the first time I had spoken in a while, and no one cared to answer. At the moment, I didn't care about the informant either—none of us did. I figured that killing him would only serve to decrease the hajji population by one, so fuck him.

Sajeeda distracted me by bringing us all chai, a hot tea that is served at any particular time, it seems, in Iraq. I had no patience for women that day.

"I am a Christian," she managed with a thick accent to me.

"Oh yeah? Christian, huh? You drink beera?"

"Oh no!"

"*Feaky-feaky?*" It was the Arabic term for "sex." She stared at me in disgust.

"No. God say pleasure with a man is bad."

"No, God likes *gahob. Ishta.*" She stared at me to see if I was joking or not in telling her God liked whores and to fuck off. Deciding I wasn't, she retreated back to the crooning of Sergeant Sellers, who was really getting going on his game, showing her how easily he could catch chickens and telling her what a great husband he would be. She wasn't even that cute, but we all had to find a way to waste away the day.

"You are very quiet." The woman wasn't particularly old, but in Iraq, people age before their time. Her hair was already graying, and wrinkles around her eyes made her look either wise or indifferent. She was sitting on a wooden bench a few feet from me and sipping from a cup of hot chai; the steam from it looped and curled around the cup, trying to survive as long as possible. She rose and sort of puttered over to me with the teapot to offer me a refill.

"Are you sick?"

"Crawford sick? Naw, fuck, he just misses his wife, wants to go home like the rest of us," Sergeant Howell interjected from his spot a few feet away. I just nodded and looked away. The old woman stood there for a few more minutes, and feeling guilty for ignoring her concerns, I picked my helmet up off the ground and showed her the picture of my wife and me inside the webbing. The night before, I had had a hell of a bad dream. Away from home, away from your wife, you get to seeing and hearing about all your buddies—their wives are fucking this and that, are pregnant, diseased, divorcing them—and your mind gets all weird. You can't think of anything else, and on this particular night, the number-one thing on my mind was my wife, or more exactly, who was with my wife. I couldn't wait to get back to the compound and call her in the hopes that she would answer. Lately, something had been wrong with her cell phone and it was becoming increasingly difficult to get ahold of her.

"Do not think of these things—it is not for a young man to worry about." The old lady turned and shuffled back to the bench she shared with our elderly interpreter. He smiled at her and lit a cheap Iraqi cigarette off of the burning embers of a butt he had just finished. After a deep puff, smoke filled the air.

"Raptor Three-two, this is God." God was our nickname for the sniper position at the stadium—a tribute to the sniper in *Navy SEALs*, a cheesy action movie that had come out when we were all kids.

"We have the target vehicle, it has stopped and the doors are open. I do not have a visual on any dismounts. Get ready, guys. Over."

"Roger, out."

"Get your shit together—this is it." Sergeant Howell spoke barely above a whisper. For what seemed like the fiftieth time, we had to force our hosts to turn off their lights in order to prevent anyone from seeing into the courtyard. We stacked against the metal gate, our breaths coming in gasps, our gear rattling almost silently—soldier noises. For the first time in my life, I remember thinking that I actually *needed* a cigarette. Whigham and I exchanged looks and hoped that we would be quick enough, and lucky enough, to take both targets. He was going to come out, peel right, while I sprinted across the narrow alley and took up a position on the far side, providing cross fire from two different positions, and also hopefully drawing any rocket fire toward me and away from the gate where the rest of the squad would be bottlenecked.

A boom shook the night air. The ground trembled, and

Sajeeda screamed a woman's scream, the kind that makes your blood curdle. *We've been compromised, they're firing at us, it's been a trick the whole time, and we're fucking dead. That's it, man, nice try, might've done something with your life, but instead you're gonna lie here and bleed in a shit-and-piss-filled alley in Baghdad.* I tried to shake off that feeling everyone gets in their gut sometimes.

A moment later, soon after noticing that I wasn't a mess of matted hair and blood, I realized the blast had been to the west about seventy-five meters away. They had attacked the compound, and right under our noses.

"Go! Go! Go!" was all I heard as I burst out the gate and into the blackness of the alley. There was nothing to be seen— the darkness was all-encompassing. My safety was off. I sprinted across to the road until my shoulder slammed into the concrete wall. The informer was full of shit; he was caught, figured out, whatever. Either way, they had changed their plans and had fired from our blind spot, right from the other side of the house we had staged in.

My eyes were adjusted and I could see Brunelle racing to the corner, still wanting the kill, but by this time the machine guns in our compound were firing, and tracers picked their way past us. The scariest thing about tracers, other than the fact that they are moving unbelievably fast, is that for every one you see, there are four bullets that you can't. I yelled for him to stop, and the second time he heard me and pulled up at the edge of the intersection. Machine-gun bullets, 7.62-millimeter, slammed into a doorway five meters past us. It was a wall of protection for our attackers. We were on one side and they were invisible on the other, escaping. Fucking headquarters fucker on the machine gun was too stupid to realize we were there. He probably didn't even know we were out there, and now he was just blindly firing as fast as he could, right at us.

In Iraq at the first sign of gunfire or excitement, every hajji within hearing distance will take to the streets like it's a spectator sport. They crowd around with children in their arms to see what the commotion is about. Searching for the miscreants in that crowd would be an exercise in futility. Disheartened, we turned north and walked back into the compound, heads down, full of anger—at hajji, at the commander, at ourselves; shit, at the world.

Sitting in the command post, I could hear Captain Sanchez laying into Sergeant Howell and Sergeant Golder: "How the fuck could you let them get away? You had every chance to catch them, what the fuck? This is your fucking fault, and now I have to get my ass reamed by the colonel for this fucked-up shit!" I let it fade out. It was all the same bullshit. I waited in line impatiently for the phone. The adrenaline began to fade behind a couple Valium.

I thought it out. Imagine a war where you can call home after a bad day. Does that make it easier, more familiar?

"Hey, honey, how was your day?"

"Oh, you know, same old stuff, killing, dying. That sort of shit. How about you?" The skeptics, the reporters, the pro- and antiwar demonstrators, they're all wrong. The news says the war's over. That was fine by us. No one else belonged there anyway. This was our war, this was my war, and it's the only one I had. I may have had my doubts about it, but it was something to hold on to. I looked forward to my phone call, knowing my wife would tell me to calm down, that it was just a dream, that there was no other man—there never are, after all.

# FIVE

# THE BANK

THE SUN CAME UP fast on those warm May mornings. First it would crest the palm trees on the far side of the Tigris, and ever so gently bright tentacles of daylight would penetrate the night in our little patch of the Fertile Crescent. The windows to our rooms were barricaded against it by planks of wood, ponchos, and sheet metal; nevertheless, a few diligent rays always found their way through the cracks and to the sleeping soldiers within.

I wearily sat up and stretched. The drab army cot creaked beneath me as I moved. I had been up most of the night patrolling, and had slept for only a few hours. My eyes still shut, I reached under my bunk and rifled through the piles of clothes, boxes, and gear until I came upon a pair of army-issue shorts. Rising, I put them on and shuffled out of the night's dreams and into the blinding light of reality that came every day.

Outside our room was a torn-up sofa someone had acquired from another part of the compound, and I plopped on it with a groan. With shaking hands I lit the day's first cigarette and inhaled deeply, followed by a violent coughing fit that had me bending over at the waist. The Iraqi cigarettes we all smoked were supremely harsh, but at fifty cents a pack, they beat the hell out of the high-priced Marlboros sold twenty miles away at Baghdad International Airport.

Most of the soldiers not on duty were still asleep, and the barracks were quiet aside from a rustling in Weapons Squad's room, where they were preparing a patrol. The locals, too, were already up and cleaning up. During the hotter months, they slept on their roofs on thin mattresses. We had taken up the habit as well, but with the arrival of electricity, and soon thereafter fans, we had moved inside shelter like the first cave dwellers.

The flies were already swarming. They started an hour or two before dawn and would alight on any exposed skin, tickling and buzzing a person awake. It was impossible to sleep in with flocks of insects on your lips and nose. I halfheartedly shook a few off of me and continued to look around, allowing myself to wake up slowly. We were on the third and final floor of our building, and from this perch I could see a city of tans and browns. Whether or not paint had ever adorned Baghdad, I don't know. The sand from the southern desert constantly blew in and covered any hint of color on the buildings.

Baghdad is composed of a bunch of tiny city-states. So many people traveled by foot that everything needed to survive was within walking distance. Women rose early and walked to the market to pick up freshly baked unleavened bread. Shop owners pawned their wares on the street corners and said their good mornings to the passersby. This gave everyone the feeling of a neighborhood. The American military, whether on purpose or not, had more or less broken these areas down into sectors, and ours split up El Maghrib and Aadhamiya. Everyone seemed to know everyone else's business within a few miles' radius—except, of course, us.

Across from our barracks was a three-story apartment building that housed several families. The women would stand up on the roof and beg for food or goods with outstretched arms. Over time, an understanding was established between them and some of the soldiers. It became commonplace to hear the ladies calling, "Renaldo!" or "Indy!" and then the beckoned soldier would send up money in a bucket from the alleyway. In exchange, the women would send down chai, or fresh food that we were unable to get any other way. It was a fairly decent relationship, and at the very least, by providing an income for our neighbors, we ensured that they benefited enough from our presence not to attack us.

The families next door were large, and a great number of children loitered about, hoping to get something from the soldiers who watched them with general disinterest. On the rooftop that morning, there were already two girls out playing. They were both young, maybe ten or eleven years old: Hida and her friend Shihead, whom we all had renamed Shithead for her tendency to throw rocks and spit on her playmates. Relative to Shithead, we all doted on Hida. You could tell she would be beautiful when she grew up. On warm evenings, she would serenade us with songs we didn't understand and bat her eyes at the soldiers who threw her candy.

Someone had taught her to play rock, paper, scissors, and although she had to hide it from the men of her household, who considered it a "boy game," for hours she would play with any soldier who showed his face, and would whine and call our names like an unsatisfied puppy if we ever left before she was done.

This morning, though, she and Shithead were putting on a play. Hida skipped back and forth along the edge of the dusty roof, clapping and singing, while Shithead narrated. Occasionally, Hida would stop and, mimicking some Hollywood star, look into an imaginary mirror and tend to her hair and makeup. I always got a laugh out of it, which was a good way to start the morning.

"What's up, Crawford? Anything exciting happen last night?" Doc Ballou dropped down onto the sofa next to me. Dust exploded, and we both coughed a bit. His Kevlar helmet slapped angrily against the faux-marble floor and his flak vest crumpled up around his neck, forcing him to tug it down in front in order to breathe. We hadn't received body armor yet, and all of us complained about the Vietnam-era flak vests, which we figured amounted to nothing but a sweaty burden that was unlikely to stop bullets anyway.

"Naw, man, just another boring night. What are you guys up to today?" My voice was flatly indifferent. The routine had worn us down. Aside from an RPG that had hit the front of our building, scaring the hell out of us, and some random sniper fire, things had been quiet since our arrival in the city, quieter than Nasiriyah or the desert.

Doc was fumbling through his gear, and eventually his hand emerged victoriously clutching a black and mild, which he lit unceremoniously. The sweet cigar smell was pungent, and the smoke hung about us like a fog of uncertainty before a gust of wind blew it away.

"We're going up to the bank past Bravo One. I don't know what the fuck for. I think the CO wants to know how much business they get or some shit." Doc was looking out at Hida's play with a smirk on his face, and he clapped and whistled when she had finished one particularly funny routine.

"Didn't you guys go to the bank yesterday?"

"Yeah, we went, but someone wasn't there or some shit. The guy we were supposed to talk to didn't come in. He's gonna be there today, I guess. It's all stupid shit anyway."

"Fucking officers want to hand up more reports, show how busy we've been." I spit into the dust. Progress here was marked by reports and reports and reports—how many teachers went to work yesterday, how long was the gas line in meters, and how many liters were sold. In this case, it was how much business does the bank do. The reports were then passed on to what we imagined was a huge pile of unread papers that someone used as fuel for bonfires or shitpaper.

"Yup" was all Doc said, and after a moment the rest of his squad began filing out of their room. Doc fingered his nine-millimeter and then rose.

"See ya later, man."

"Yeah, you guys take it easy, all right?" With that Doc began the long descent down the three flights of concrete stairs, his left hand on the railing, his right holding his Kevlar headpiece like a football helmet. As Weapons Squad passed by, they all said their good mornings. Mitchell stopped to try to grab me in a quick headlock, but I quickly slapped it away.

"What's up, fucker?"

"Nothing, man, about to go back to sleep. Hey, wake me up for chow when you get back, okay?"

"You know it, man. See you in a few hours."

"Yeah, you guys have fun."

"Fuck, you know us. It'll take us two fucking hours just to get to the bank, the way Pybus leads these patrols. Mother-fucker sees his shadow around every corner."

Mears came out of the room and yelled at Mitchell to get moving.

"What, do you think you're the cheer-tator here or some-thing?" Mitchell spat at him.

Mears had received the movie *Bring It On* from someone back home a few days before, and with a lack of other enter-tainment options, the two had already watched it a half-dozen times.

"That's right, and I make the cheer-cisions and I'll deal with the cheer-onsequences," Mears spat right back. I never understood how it became one of his favorite movies, but everyone had their own tastes, and I certainly had different ideas than Mears. No matter what the situation was, he never became disillusioned with the American mission in Iraq. Whenever the rest of us would voice our doubts, he would staunchly defend the war and all its intricacies.

Mitchell gave me a quick jab in the shoulder that I was too tired to respond to, and headed down the stairs. I watched them fumble away with their weapons and heavy gear. I took one last drag off my cigarette and then flicked it away into the alley to join the thousands of other butts that littered the ground. I turned toward my squad's room, and as the door closed behind me, I heard Hida begin her screams of protest at the lack of an audience.

The rooms were all near pitch dark because of the window coverings, and aside from the few rays of sunlight that I already mentioned, they resembled very cluttered and musky caves. I moved slowly and cautiously so as not to disturb any of my slumbering comrades. Their snores created a symphony to sleep to, and before long I'd be joining them in their sleepy fantasies of home—while somewhere outside, Weapons Squad was heading toward their own nightmare.

I was almost asleep again and I didn't hear Sergeant Golder come into the room looking for me. It wasn't until he gave my cot a nudge with his boot that I became aware of the giant looming over me.

"What?" I asked, annoyed at being pulled back from the brink.

"Hey, Crawford, we're going out to the Ministry of Labor. I need a guy from your team on the gun."

"Aww, isn't there anyone awake?" I pleaded.

"Nope. Pick someone and have them down in the motor pool in five minutes."

"Roger, Sar'nt."

Having forced me to concede defeat, Golder made his way out of the room, he, too, carefully dancing to avoid disturbing the resting bodies strewn about like some apocalyptic disaster scene. I wiped the sleep from my eyes and sat up. I always hated volunteering people. If someone got fucked, then that was the way things were, but picking them for something I didn't want to do always gave me a pang of guilt.

Farmer was never a morning person, and I didn't feel like dealing with the argument that would ensue if I awoke him. He was a good soldier, and undoubtedly would go, but not before I heard all about the oppression his people had endured for hundreds of years. It was too early to deal with that, and if I wasn't willing to send him just out of convenience, then I couldn't very well send Pearson, either.

"Screw it." I reached for a uniform, still drenched with sweat from the night before, and, cringing, I slipped on the soiled clothes, careful to hold my breath as they passed by my nose. After a few minutes of searching in the dark for my flak vest and helmet, I headed out the door, this time neglecting to be careful of my sleeping friends. On my way down the stairs, I stopped in Weapons Squad's empty room and grabbed an M-240 machine gun and a box of 7.62 ammunition. Hida waved, and I smiled despite my annoyance.

Down at the vehicles, Sergeant Golder was already waiting with Sergeant Gilleon.

"Hurry up and get that gun up, Crawford," Golder said, more out of habit than urgency.

"Roger, Sar'nt. Where we going?" I asked as I climbed into the back of a cargo Humvee. The mount was an Iraqi military gate we had rammed, the bars welded together and bolted onto the frame of our vehicle. The machine gun slid into place with a clang. I squirted some oil into the weapon and, after riding the charging handle back and forth a few times, loaded it and slapped the feed tray cover down.

"Out to the MOL to see Bravo Company's first sergeant. We're gonna go see if we can't barter for some more vehicles, because two of ours broke down yesterday. You ready to go?"

"Let's do it," I said, slapping the top of the Humvee. Golder squeezed into the driver's seat and out the back gate we went, gravel flying behind us. I stood in the back, using the gun for balance as I absentmindedly swung it left and right at potential targets. It was a ten- or fifteen-minute drive through fairly busy traffic. There was no opposition, as usual, and my main occupation was simply pointing the weapon at oncoming traffic in order to entice them to stop as we cruised through red lights and traffic jams. Iraqi commuters going our way seized the opportunity and trailed behind us like crude ambulance chasers eager to gain a few minutes on their drive.

Bravo Company was housed at the MOL, a large office building on the western edge of our sector. With a wave, we were through their gate and pulling up to the main entrance to the building. A few soldiers sat outside in T-shirts, their rifles leaning casually beside them as they shaved or brushed their teeth in the morning light. We came to a stop, and Golder turned in his seat and faced me.

"Monitor the radio. We'll be back in a few minutes."

"Roger, Sar'nt."

Gilleon and Golder walked past the soldiers without a word, and I settled down in the back, taking my vest off one shoulder to get to the MRE that was in my butt pack.

I had just settled down for some breakfast meat loaf and gravy when I heard static break over the radio. I took off my Kevlar helmet and pressed the mike to my ear. There was only silence, but just as I settled back to my meal, it broke squelch again.

"Three-four, this is Raptor Main—say again, over." It was the company commander's radio operator back in the compound. They were talking to my platoon's Weapons Squad. We must have been too far away to hear the entire conversation, and all that came out of the speaker were broken and distorted responses.

"Three-four, I need you to calm down. What is your grid? Over." A chill ran down my spine and I snapped on the plastic MRE spoon dangling between my teeth. Sweat ran down my cheek, tickling it, and I quickly wiped my face, all my senses intent on what was going on in my ear.

"Three-four, this is Raptor Main. Say again, how many personnel are hit? Over." That was it. I dropped the hand mike and flung myself out of the back of the Humvee, losing my footing on the tailgate and coming down on both knees on the concrete parking lot. The Bravo Company soldiers smirked only briefly as I broke into a sprint coming into the building.

"Sar'nt Golder! Sar'nt Golder!" I was frantic. From what I had heard, things were bad; I imagined them pinned down under a hail of gunfire. I finally found the two platoon sergeants standing around a few Humvees behind the building. The Bravo Company first sergeant was playing the part of used-car salesman, seeing what was the best deal he could get for these vehicles.

"Crawford, what—"

"Sar'nt, Weapons Squad was just hit. I don't know how bad, but they're on the radio."

"Where are they at?" Golder asked, suddenly going into action.

"They were going to the bank by Bravo One, but I don't know where they are now!" I was chasing after Gilleon and Golder now, at a dead run, and was barely on board when the engine roared to life and I was slammed onto my back in the bed of the Humvee.

"Hold on, Crawford!" was all Golder managed to yell back at me, and he certainly didn't wait for an answer. Gilleon was in the front seat, cradling his rifle and cursing at the top of his lungs. We went out the front gate, almost knocking down the guard there, and our tires squealed and smoked as Sergeant Golder executed a tight left turn across traffic and into the other lane. I fell down again, slamming my shoulder onto the railing of the Humvee. There was nothing to hold on to in the back except for the machine gun, and I clung to it to avoid being thrown out.

In and out of traffic we weaved, onto sidewalks, through people's yards, into oncoming traffic. I hung on like a terrified kid on a roller coaster. I could hear myself yelling and cursing, not just at the traffic blocking us but at the whole situation. I wasn't sure what the three of us could do if there was a problem bad enough that a rifle squad couldn't handle it, but we certainly weren't going to be left out.

By this time I was beginning to get my balance, so when we turned the last corner I quickly recovered, and ahead I saw a crowd of hajjis pressing in. We flew over the curb, where there were American soldiers kneeling behind corners and cars. In the street I saw pools of blood. Blood everywhere.

I looked over to my right and saw a soldier I knew leaning up against the bank, his muzzle creeping around the corner as he watched an alleyway. He looked at me, and I yelled.

"Hey, what you got!?" He just stared back blindly like I wasn't there. "Hey! What the fuck am I looking for!?" I desperately wanted a description of the target, or at least a direction, but the soldier wasn't even there, at least not mentally. He just stared at me, his face pale.

Specialist Mears came running up to me, the radio bouncing awkwardly on his back.

"Crawford, you got a first-aid bandage?" His voice was urgent but still in control, and without thinking I tossed him mine.

"What am I looking for, Mears?" I asked as he bustled away.

"Anything, everything," was all he yelled back, and though I didn't feel like this was much help, at least I knew someone was awake.

---

WHEN WEAPONS SQUAD had left that morning for their patrol, there was no ill wind in the air. Their hearts were filled with apathy and their minds with the breakfast that awaited them back at the compound. Specialist Pybus walked point and the rest of the squad trailed behind. Mears and Mitchell had hung toward the rear, their constant disaffected banter separating them from their team leaders' gung-ho attitude. They had been to the bank the day before, but someone was missing—the interpreter, or maybe the bank manager. No one really cared to learn the whole story. It was just another daily chore. What they hadn't figured on was that by making an appointment to see the bank manager, they had effectively let the bad guys know when and where they would be at a particular time.

Down a dirty sidewalk beside the four-lane road they walked, hunched over slightly in a staggered line. Though it was still morning, sweat dripped into their eyes, and it was hard not to stare at the ground under the increasing weight of their helmets. Old cars careened at breakneck speed through the busy street, clouds of smog swirling behind them. Occasionally, small children would beg them for money or candy. By this time only Mears still had the patience for it all, and he would often be found reaching awkwardly underneath his gear and into his pocket for small pieces of MRE candy that no one would have eaten anyway.

As they passed through the market, the shopkeepers eyed them warily before nodding their heads in greeting. Great piles of skinned and boiled sheep heads kept watch on the street, their faces given the illusion of movement by the swarms of flies that alighted on them.

"How do you think they cook that shit?" Mears asked no one in particular.

"Probably in soup or something. Fucking nasty, ain't it?" Mitchell called back, fighting an urge to pick one up and use it like a puppet.

Occasionally, a young woman would pass by in her schoolgirl uniform and dare a slight smile, prompting catcalls. Most times they enjoyed the attention and would wink back or smile broadly, as long as there weren't any men near them. The language of sex is the same in every country.

"What the fuck?" Mitchell asked with a fervent shake of his head and a downward swing of his rifle.

"Why are we fucking stopping again?" Mears answered with his own question as he bent over at the waist, changing the position of the radio on his back. The hand mike was attached to the chinstrap of his helmet, allowing him to hear everything immediately. Of all the radio operators I have met, he was among the best.

At the head of the column, Pybus had stopped the movement and was now peering cautiously at the other side of the road. He was well known as the most paranoid member of the platoon. The other soldiers made fun of Weapons Squad for that. It was a daily occurrence for them to stop and berate a passerby for whistling, thinking he might be signaling. Or the best was the suspicion that someone was pacing them, as if that were a great secret, as if somewhere under the city, deep inside a bunker, Iraqi insurgents were plotting an attack based

on American pace count. It was silly and added to the lack-
adaisical attitude of some of the squad, but all in all, every
time they took fire, they realized it was always better to be too
cautious than too reckless.

From the back, Mears struggled to hear what was going
on. His call sign on the platoon radio was Fat Kid, although
he wasn't particularly overweight, just a slight jiggle along the
belt line. His blond hair and wire-rimmed glasses made him
look much more like a freshman in college than a soldier, but
he was always on top of things, and although we had our dis-
agreements about tactics and politics, it was always nice to
know he was with you on patrol. Mears groaned aloud and
turned to Mitchell.

"Did you hear that?"

"Naw, what's going on?" Mitchell asked from his spot as
rear guard. He was on a knee, trying to lean some of the weight
he was carrying against a large stone wall while still pulling security.

"Fucking Pybus said he saw some kid walk toward them,
stop, tie his shoe, and then turn down an alley. He thinks we
should chase him."

"Tell me Sergeant Tibbets isn't listening to him." Mitchell
groaned.

"I don't know. I can't hear him."

Satisfied that the enemy had moved out and that the path
was now clear, Pybus continued on, an unhappy procession
following behind him. Up ahead, past the unused playground
adorned with Disney characters, lay the bank. It stood unob-
trusively on an intersection surrounded by furniture stores

whose gaudy wares cluttered the sidewalk. As they neared the entrance, Tibbets yelled back.

"Doc, you and Harris stay outside and pull security. The rest of you come with me." Doc and Harris exchanged pitiful sighs, followed by halfhearted attempts to change their fate. The bank was air-conditioned, and even a few moments of climate-controlled respite was relished. One by one, the squad filed up the steps into the near-empty bank, leaving their two guards standing alone on the sidewalk.

Hunting for shade in the busy street was never easy, but Harris found an overhang in front of the bank and seated himself on the curb, his rifle leaning across his knees, his right hand grasping the pistol grip. Doc Ballou sat to his left and watched through squinted eyes as Harris lit a cigarette and exhaled smoke into the grimy air. All around them, civilians moved as if unaware of the occupying army seated at their feet. It was a busy day in a busy city. If Doc and Harris had been looking for it, they might have noticed that for once there were no children hovering about, but we hadn't been in Baghdad long enough to learn those lessons yet.

Inside the bank, Tibbets and the interpreter talked to the manager while Mears called up the bank numbers on the radio. Their weapons hung off them, and helmets were strewn about on the counter or floor. The soldiers were busy enjoying the cool air.

Mitchell leaned against a wall, talking to Castillo about a girl back home who had sent him her journal outlining her undying love and devotion toward him. Castillo listened absentmindedly, laughing at all the good parts, but everyone's mind was elsewhere. The bank wasn't very far from the compound, and the patrol had the feel of a casual Sunday-afternoon stroll.

Then the crashing sound of gunfire was right outside the bank. Everyone turned toward the door. Mitchell was closest, and he sprung to the entrance, his weapon shouldered, his Kevlar left lying on the floor. He rushed outside but froze in the doorway, the breath knocked out of him. At his feet lay Doc, legs twitching in protest, trying to get up and run. His hands had a stranglehold on his own neck, and spurts of blood poured from between his fingers. Doc's mouth opened and closed, but no words came out.

Harris was up, still on a knee, his rifle at his shoulder. Twenty meters away, a hajji dressed in black and carrying a nine-millimeter pistol fled toward a waiting red Volkswagen Passat. Harris fired once, then twice more in succession. The attacker spun around, carried by the impact of bullets in his chest and head. By the second shot, only momentum kept him on his feet; his arms flailed at his side and his head hung limply on his gaping chest. Before anyone else could react, he was down, lifeless in a pool of his own blood.

Mitchell reached into the doorway for his helmet and then stormed into the street to Harris's side. Glancing down at Doc, he couldn't look at anything but the symmetrical wound in his throat. Blood continued to spurt out with each struggle of his heart, and Doc's face was pale with death.

*Shit! Shit! Shit!* was all Mitchell could think, but there was no time to ponder deeper thoughts than that anyway. The red Passat was already tearing away down the street. At Harris's side, he ran to the dead Iraqi in the street, his rifle on fire, ready to finish the man off if he had any fight left in him. They grabbed the pistol from his dead hand. All the king's horses and all the king's men couldn't put this hajji back together again.

Pybus was already on Doc when they turned around. He had dragged him closer to the building and imaginary safety.

"Doc, you're gonna be okay. No problem, right?" he sputtered out nervously as he applied pressure directly to the wound on his friend's neck.

"Mears, get on the radio!" he yelled, but it was already being done.

"Raptor Main, this is Raptor Three-four. We've been hit at the bank! We need a medevac immediately! Over."

"Three-four, this is main. Calm down—what's your grid? Over."

"We're at the fucking bank! You have the grid written on the wall right in front of you! We need a medevac fucking NOW! Doc is hit bad! Over."

The company commander, his staff, and his radio operators very rarely left the compound. They didn't know the streets. If any of the regular soldiers had been in the CP, it would have been as simple as "We're across from the furniture store" or "Go out the front gate and take a left," but that wasn't the case. Paperwork had to be filed, grids had to be copied and sent to higher.

The Quick Reaction Force was immediately called up, and within moments word had spread throughout Third Platoon that one of our squads was in trouble. At the compound, every soldier was downstairs in minutes, their gear and weapons ready for command, but none came. They stood, shifting their weight from one foot to the other, bitching about the delay. Almost forty-five minutes would go by before any American soldiers left the compound as a rescue team. Even when they did, some of the squads, piecemealed from different platoons, took longer routes or were on the wrong frequencies.

Back at the bank, Mears was still yelling into the radio but receiving only opposition from officers who couldn't comprehend the situation. One officer on battalion staff threatened to pursue disciplinary action against him for cursing on the radio. Everything was black-and-white in the CP. They never seemed to realize that we weren't there to write reports or to have soccer games with the locals.

Long before any of our own medics arrived at the scene, the Iraqi police came with their own ragtag ambulance, held together by rust and peeling blue paint. An overweight hajji with a mustache hurried to the dead Iraqi and began to put him on a stretcher.

"Leave that fucker there and get over here!" Mitchell yelled to a few policemen who were assisting the first man in dragging the body. Private Buchanan had his hands over his mouth and was staring at the whole scene, trying not to hyperventilate. Mears grabbed him bodily by the shoulders and shook him.

"Get the fuck over there and pull security!" There was no doubt who was in charge. While everyone else stood numbly by, a young specialist from Tallahassee Community College with no military experience other than the Florida National Guard organized a perimeter and communicated with higher.

––––––

I WAS HERE NOW, looking out for "anything and everything." Mears had wrapped my bandage around Doc's neck and was hurriedly debriefing Platoon Sergeants Gilleon and Golder. They realized that a medevac was too far away to help, so they loaded Doc Ballou's near-lifeless body into the back of the Iraqi ambulance. Pybus jumped in too, still tending to Doc's pulsating neck. Someone yelled at the driver, who was busy trying to retrieve the corpse from the middle of the road, and he too jumped in.

"What the fuck happened?" Mitchell finally asked Harris.

"We were just sitting there and this guy walks right up to us, pulls out a pistol, and shoots us." Harris spoke a southern twang that divulged no real emotion or effect.

"Us? What do you mean, us?" Mitchell asked, now eye-balling Harris.

Pointing at a small hole in the center of his flak vest, Harris explained, "Oh, I took a shot too, right here, but it don't hurt none." Blood was beginning to show darkly on the camouflage pattern.

"Shit, man, I guess it's not that bad, 'cause you're up and walking, but what the fuck do I know? You need to get in that ambulance."

"Naw, man, I'm okay."

"You're getting the fuck up in that ambulance. Now!"

"Gawd-dawg, man, I shot that fucker."

"Harris, you gotta get in the ambulance." Mitchell was trying to take him by the arm, but Harris protested.

"Gawd-dawg, man, I'm all right! Boy, you know he's dead. I got him good."

"Yeah, man, you did. Now, come on, you gotta get up here." Harris finally gave in and loaded up with Doc.

"Crawford, we're moving. We have to escort that ambulance back!" Golder yelled as he jumped into the driver's seat once more and I put my attention to the gun again. Sergeant Gilleon stayed behind to organize the squad's movements.

We took off with the ambulance right behind us. It took only a moment to get back to the compound, and we cursed at the guard, who was taking his time opening the wire gate. Before the vehicle was even completely stopped, I was jumping out of the back, running toward the ambulance.

The Iraqi medic opened the door and attempted to pull out the stretcher carrying Doc, but Sergeant Golder shoved him unceremoniously out of the way. This was our man, and the way we figured it, the last thing Doc needed was to see some hajji leaning over him. The two of us grabbed the stretcher and ran the last few meters into the aid station with him.

"You're okay, buddy, you're fine." Golder spoke words of encouragement, and so did I, but mine were hollow. His eyes flitted around unseeing, and his face had the hue of a corpse. *Not a chance in hell*, I thought. We put the stretcher onto a stand and were just as quickly pushed away by the medics.

It was then that I noticed Harris standing a few feet away in his brown T-shirt. There was a nickel-sized hole in the breast of it, and a large bloodstain all down the front. Still, he looked unconcerned and puffed on a cigarette.

"Holy shit, man, you are too fucking hard! What the fuck?" I exclaimed with awe.

"Gawd-dawg, man, it's not that bad. My vest stopped most of it—just broke the skin, that's all." And he was right: Within a few days, Harris was back on duty with a large purplish-black bruise across the right side of his chest—and one hell of a story.

The event was all but over, but the adrenaline was still pumping strong. I stood there with Harris, unsure of what to do, when Sergeant Golder grabbed me by the arm and yanked me back to the Humvee.

"Red Passat!" was all he said as I crawled back onto the gun. Back out the gate we went, joined now by the ill-timed rescue operation. All over the sector, soldiers were stopping red Volks-wagens. They searched them, knocked out the windows, and slashed the tires, anything to make them feel like they had achieved some form of vengeance, but we caught no one.

It took Doc almost an hour to get on a Black Hawk heli-copter and off to a mobile army hospital unit. The company commander claimed Third Infantry Division had messed up copying the nine-line medevac request, but none of us be-lieved that the mix-up had been on their side. The bullet had missed Doc's jugular by millimeters and had traveled down, lodging itself in one of his lungs. He lost that one along with forty pounds, but ended up recovering pretty well—and never had to patrol with Harris again.

That night we had a company meeting, where the battalion commander and the chaplain tried to speak words of encouragement to worried and angry soldiers. We were a team, they said. They told us to persevere and stay strong. Every soldier is important to the chain of command, and they were suffering right beside us. It was a good speech, but when the time came, neither the chaplain nor the battalion commander could remember the names of either of our soldiers who were hit.

# SIX

# CUM

M UD SPLASHED UP the boy's body with every footfall, and plumes of it followed behind him as he ran ever faster. His filthy T-shirt heaved with every labored breath. Spindly legs weaved in and out of the trash piles, avoiding the more menacing ones. Behind locks of greasy black hair were fearful eyes, glancing back every few moments at the gang of bigger kids that pressed closer with every moment. A step faltered and he stumbled, sliding hard on the pavement.

I watched all this with mild interest. It had so far been a long day, and any entertainment was welcome. I was leaning casually against a mud-brick wall behind a gas station. There were two in our sector, the Amoco and the BP. Neither had any affiliation with the actual companies—those were just nicknames we used to separate them. Today, I was at the BP and, leaning against that wall, watching the heat dance off of gasoline-soaked pavement. The scene unfolding before me passed for quality entertainment.

I had watched the kid through a large wrought-iron gate that hung precariously on the wall that surrounded three sides of the station. To the front was a busy four-lane highway from which traffic swarmed in a sea of horn-blowing and yelling. They surged in, trying to be the next in line for a full tank of benzene. The lines were always long, down the road, around the corner; kilometers away was the back. People slept in line, ate in line, and, most often, stewed in their discontent there.

Local scalpers welded extra tanks into beat-up trucks and cars and filled them up to the rim, only to sell them for insanely inflated prices around the corner. The ones we caught risked getting their jerry cans full of gas sliced open and thrown into the street. The station workers themselves charged extra, and allowed friends and relatives to skip through again and again. We had no interpreters and couldn't even read the stated price of the gasoline, let alone resolve any of the countless arguments that took place. The whole situation was a mess, and the lack of fuel came to represent the failure of the Coalition. And, with American soldiers stationed there day and night, immobile, we presented an easy target for taunts, insults, and the occasional bullet.

The kid was up again and running, this time not so fast; his knees and palms were bloody from the fall, and I could see he was limping. The half-dozen or so boys chasing him also must have sensed his weakness, and they intensified the chase, gaining two steps for every one he took. The end was near, I could tell, and to my delight it looked like the pinnacle of the hunt was going to happen right behind the gate, where I could watch all the action.

"Hey, Sellers, come check this shit out."

"What is it?"

"Dude, this kid is about to get his ass kicked." They were close now, just out of arm's reach, and I knew at any moment there would be a scream and a great pile of mud and dirt would rise around the catch. But the little boy surprised me. At the last second, just as an angry hand was reaching for his shoulder, he cut over and slid under the gate, coming to a rest right at the toes of my boots.

Through dark sunglasses I looked down at him, impassive. His eyes were large and brown, and they begged for help.

"Gotta stop running one day, boy" was what my daddy used to say, and I figured it was true in any country. The bullies packed up against the gate, unsure of what to do. For all I cared, they could have the kid. I didn't give a shit what happened to any of them. A rock, aimed at the still-prostrate boy at my feet, skipped off of asphalt and bounced harmlessly off my shin.

"Hey, motherfucker! You wanna throw fucking rocks?!" I took a step toward the gate and reached out with gloved hands to grab one of them. Robbed of their prey, they bolted away, glancing back every few moments to show their disdain.

The kid was on his feet and grabbed at my sleeve. I slapped his hand away.

"Don't fucking touch me! Grubby little bastard!"

"Mistah. Mistah. *Shukran.*"

"Yeah, you're welcome. Go away now. *Imshe!* Go home." But he wouldn't leave; he just followed me around.

"Mistah, *Shishmek*, Cum." He pointed to his chest proudly.

"Dude, your name is Cum? I'd pick on you too, man. That fucking sucks."

"Yes. Yes! Cum!" He jumped up and down with excitement. I tried to shoo him away for a while, then I resorted to simply ignoring him. I stood in the sun all that day with Cum by my side. He imitated my every move, and anytime I pointed at someone and yelled, he would do the same in Arabic. He kept this up for hours until I finally broke down.

"You speak any English, Cum?"

He cocked his head to one side and then answered. "Yes, mistah! Cum!"

Across the street, I saw a kid towing a cooler behind him. Those were the Pepsi vendors, selling Arabic sodas for inflated prices. I held out a dollar to my wide-eyed friend and with the other hand pointed across the street.

"Cum, two Pepsi, one dollar. Okay?" I held up two fingers and pointed again, then handed away the dollar.

With a spring in his step, the filthy little street kid scampered across the road, returning at the same pace with two cold sodas. I took one and indicated the other was for him. He cradled it with both hands and, smiling approvingly at me, began to speak in Arabic.

"Yeah, whatever, Cum. Drink your fucking Pepsi." Despite my reluctance, I had been adopted.

Cum was only nine or ten years old, and his clothes hung loosely off of emaciated shoulders and arms. His hair was matted and dirty and in need of being cut. Yellow teeth broke up the gaps in his mouth. He was altogether a pitiful sight.

"He sure ain't winning no beauty contests, is he?" Sellers had pointed out with a laugh upon meeting him. The kid was legitimately homeless. There was no rosy future in a capitalist Iraq for Cum; he was at the bottom of the world and everyone around him knew it.

The days were long at the BP station, but Cum never got tired of standing in the sun with me. Every so often he would reach for my helmet, and if no one was around I would humor him by taking it off and showing the picture in the webbing. It was taken with my wife in New Orleans. To me it was a glimpse of the past; to him, nothing more than a fantasy, a beautiful woman, nice clothes, America, happiness. He'd stare at it with dreamy eyes and then smile at me and try to put on the helmet.

"Naw, buddy . . . you and I both know you got lice and shit," I'd say as nicely as possible while I reached for my Kevlar. It never hurt his feelings, the things I'd say. Cum spoke virtually no English when we met, and even at the end, he could communicate only in a few broken phrases whose meaning was always unclear.

Our one-sided conversations made the days go faster. I would tell him about fishing in the St. Johns River with my friends when I was his age, and he would tell me whatever it was he told me. Either way, he loved the company, and I guess I didn't mind too much either. Before long, he was working for me. I'd give him money to go get us both lunch, and off he would scamper. In a snap he'd be back, his grubby hands clutching plastic bags full of kabobs. Mine were just as filthy, so it usually didn't bother me, though at times all I could think of was that he, like most of the lower-income Arabs, wiped his ass with his hand. I brought him a roll of toilet paper one day, and after a while of trying to show him how to use it through rudimentary signaling, I just gave up, much to the humor of those around us. For Christmas I bought him some kind of ten-dollar video-game system that someone was selling. I was pretty sure it wouldn't work, but he was so adamant that it was what he wanted, I just couldn't resist. I suppose I just wanted to feel like it wasn't all just a waste.

Before long, he had been adopted by the rest of the squad, too. The workers at the gas station hired him to clean up, although I'm not sure they paid him. Of all the Iraqis I met during my tour, Cum was the only one who displayed what is seen as the idealistic Western work ethic. He was at that damn BP station at six in the morning and stayed all day, sweeping, picking up trash, or running errands. He didn't sit in the shade and sip chai, play with other kids, or do the general fucking off that kids his age do.

Having him around began to prove useful. Whenever arguments would break out between Iraqis, Cum was, absurdly enough, both the interpreter and witness for most of them, and his word was usually taken over even the most eloquent of suspects. Rarely did we have an official interpreter, and even those had questionable motives. Cum just wanted to please us. "What, Cum? You say this guy did it? Well, fuck him, then."

And with that we would snatch whoever was implicated and either evict or arrest them.

He was a good kid, but it took a while to realize how attached he had become to us. One day, too sick to patrol, I stayed in the compound. Cum saw our squad approaching without me and, assuming the worst, ran off crying. The next day when I saw him, he ran up and hugged me.

"All right, Cum, don't get so touchy, man."

"He thought you were dead," the interpreter told me, and looking at the happiness in the boy's eyes, I figured he was okay in my book. After that I began to bring him portions of MREs that I didn't eat; and when anonymous care packages came, I would rummage through for cheap toys that he might want.

The biggest contribution we made to Cum's quality of life was as his protector. Any time an adult berated him, they stood a very high chance of receiving an instant scolding from one of us. More than once, I had to slap a bully on the back of the head and send him running. The neighborhood kids knew he was homeless, and they tortured him relentlessly.

Those days were too hot and long to distinguish between, and I don't know how long I knew the kid—I guess maybe four months—before it happened. I was standing there, watching the sun dance off the collage of rusty cars and donkey carts, when Cum came running up to me with a Christmas-morning smile on his face.

"John! John! Cum's sister!" He pointed back to the large gate that stood guard at the back of the BP. Behind it was a great expanse of dirt that ran clear across the sector. It was where I had first seen him running. Used as an impromptu landfill, the lot was also rumored to harbor caches of weapons beneath the surface, although none were ever found or even searched for.

Between the gate and the field ran a small dirt-covered alleyway lined with small huts, mud walls engulfing them and their small courtyards in typical Iraqi fashion. Standing on the far side of the gate, just outside the station parking lot, were five or six women, most old, one young. Cum grabbed my hand and tugged me over there.

"Sellers, c'mere, man. Let's walk back over there. Cum wants to introduce us to his sister," I said with the kind of grin a man has only when, well, he's about to meet someone's sister.

"His sister, huh?" Sellers answered with a laugh. "All right, man, let's go meet the family."

So we trekked back to the waiting women. They wore smiles along with traditional robes that covered everything but their faces. The older ladies were all in black, and the young one was decked out like a statue of the Virgin Mary. Her white and blue robe was accented by a white head scarf. At nineteen or twenty, she was strikingly beautiful.

When I got closer, she looked down with dark eyes and I could see she was blushing in spite of her amber skin. Black locks of hair cradled her cheekbones and trickled down onto thin shoulders. She was by far the best-looking woman I had seen in months.

I immediately became aware of the two-day beard I had. It had been days since I had brushed my teeth, and weeks since I had bathed.

"Sister, Leena." Cum breathed a sigh of satisfaction and watched as Leena and I squared off awkwardly.

"Hi, how are you ladies doing?" I sputtered to the group, grinning like a fool, then focusing on Leena. "What's up with you, girl?" Since most of the women we encountered spoke little or no English, cheesy lines had become the norm. Catcalling was a fun and mostly harmless way to relieve stress. Leena's blush darkened even more, and I could see her begin to smile. Her lips parted ever so slightly as she looked up at me.

"I am fine, how are you?" She had a slight British accent that somehow made her more attractive.

"Where did you learn English?" I asked, my heart in my throat. Cum and the other women all stood listening approvingly to a conversation they couldn't understand.

"I studied at the university before the war. Now it's too dangerous to go there," she answered without hesitation.

"Shit, I know where that is. We'll walk you to school anytime you like," Sellers jumped in.

"So you're Cum's sister?" I ignored my friend and his less-than-honorable intentions.

"No, he just tells people that. He has no family, but sometimes I take care of him. Like you do."

The oldest of the women gestured to Leena and then to me with a toothless smile.

"That is my grandmother," Leena stated matter-of-factly as her eyes continued to bore into my soul. The woman stepped forward and ever so gingerly reached out a hand to me, palm facing the sky. After a brief moment, I took it and shook her hand. The old woman looked confused and then began to laugh. Turning to the other women, she spoke quickly in Arabic. They would gesture occasionally to Leena or me. It was a heated conversation, and all of a sudden I realized what was happening.

"Holy shit, Sellers, I think they want us to hook up. She probably wanted a dowry payment sort of thing—they do that shit over here I think." I spoke in a low voice so Leena wouldn't hear me.

"Well, shit, man, you can have four wives in Iraq. I say do it—this bitch is smoking." You can always trust your friends for good advice.

The women had finished their conversation and the grandmother again reached out, this time grasping my arm above the elbow and gently tugging me in an attempt to get me through a hole in the gate. Cum pushed me from behind, but I stalled. I shook them off, pulled off my Kevlar helmet, and showed the women the picture of my wife that I kept there and then gestured to my ring finger.

"You are married, America?" one of the women asked in broken English.

"Yes, ma'am."

"This is not America," she pointed out, and I didn't have an answer for that.

"Leena?" I asked.

"They want you to come to our house and eat," she answered, clearly embarrassed as hell. It was still midday, and the heat kept the streets empty. They gestured to a house less than a hundred yards from us. I looked at Sellers, and he urged me on.

"Hey, I'm not going alone—he has to come with me," I said, and Sellers agreed with a nod. When we both started forward, the old woman stopped and pointed just to me. Leena spoke for her.

"She says just you." She looked disappointed when I failed to move any farther.

"Tell her I'm sorry, I'm not gonna wander around out here alone. Someone will try to kill me." Leena spoke quickly in Arabic to her family, and the old woman released my arm and with a disdainful look turned on her heels and headed back to her home. The other women all followed, but as Leena moved away, I reached out and touched her arm through the gate.

I could feel the warmth of her skin beneath her sleeve, and she turned to look back. We were close now, maybe a foot apart, and I could smell perfume on her.

"Wait, is that where you live? Can I come see you sometime?" I asked. Leena smiled like someone who knows they're doing something bad but doesn't give a damn.

"I am in the third house on the left, and yes, you can come see me again." As she skipped off to join the others, Cum looked disappointed, but I was all smiles. I hadn't been that close to a woman in six months. The guilt I should have felt was muted by questions about the validity of my own relationship. I told myself that just because I was married didn't mean my wife was. It was a joke that wasn't much comfort when the teenaged hookers came by advertising their wares.

Sellers was laughing at me as we walked back to our position. Whalee, a local shop owner, sauntered up with a wry grin.

"Very beautiful woman, yes?" Whalee was shady, but likable.

"What was that all about? I think the grandmother wanted money or something," I said, and Whalee stifled a laugh.

"Of course, my friend, you are right, she wanted to marry you. You are smart for not going. It is too dangerous for you to go anywhere alone. Forget her. If you want a girl, you ask me and I will get you one." This started us on a whole new tangent of going rates for *gahob*s, and where the best *feaky-feaky* could be found.

But I didn't forget about Leena, and before long everyone in the squad knew about the proposal. Cum went from some kid to family. "Hey, Crawford, where's your little brother? I want some chicken for lunch." Before long, it became commonplace to stop by Leena's house whenever we patrolled the area. We would walk by and the neighborhood children would run out and we would stop, kneel, and play with them quickly, tickling or teasing them. I would stand in the street and talk to Leena through a door she would hold ajar. We'd talk about the music she liked, school, what America was like, the usual things. I began to look forward to those quick meetings. By the end of a month, she would meet me by the gate behind the gas station and bring chai to drink. More often than not it would be burnt, but I always pretended not to notice and asked for seconds.

While Cum watched from afar, we would stand and talk for twenty minutes or so and then I would walk back to work and she would go back home. I knew she was aglow with dreams of an American husband and an American lifestyle. I, on the other hand, had no intentions of marriage, but I did enjoy the conversations. It was like being home, even if only for brief moments. Her smile was infectious, and her laughter sounded to me like flowers growing.

As the intolerable summer turned cooler, Leena continued to bring me chai, sometimes flowers, or a tape player with Phil Collins or *NSYNC on it, and we would talk about American music. I was of the distinct opinion that Iraqis had some bad taste in music.

On one such day, a shiny black SUV rolled behind her on the street. It slowed to a crawl and then stopped past us on the road. Immediately wary, I took a step back, masking my profile behind a concrete wall, my weapon at the ready. The eyes in the driver's seat never left mine, and there was hate buried in them.

"No, John," Leena chided me.

"What's his problem?"

"That is my cousin, he does not like Americans, and he wants to marry me. I cannot stand him, but you cannot hurt him, either. I will take care of it and be right back."

She nervously walked up to the car. An argument in Arabic ensued, and although I couldn't understand the language, the scene was familiar enough. After a moment, her cousin grabbed her arm and snatched her into the vehicle. I took a step forward, but a quick glance from Leena told me that it was not the time for action. Defeated, I went back to my position.

A week went by before we went to that side of town again, and as I stood there, wondering when Leena would come calling, a young man wandered by and struck up a conversation with Sellers and me. Before long the conversation turned to sex, unremarkably; that's the one favorite topic of both Iraqi men and American soldiers.

"I know a *gahob* that lives near here. She likes Americans. I saw her with a soldier having *feaky-feaky*," the teenager boasted while demonstrating lewd gestures. This sort of behavior was normal. Women only had to be seen once smiling or talking to an American, and what reputation they had was gone immediately. That was the case here, I was sure. "I have had her too, very good, yes?"

I laughed at the kid and asked where she lived.

"Behind the benzene station. Her name is Leena." I stared at him, first in disbelief and then in anger.

"And you saw her with two American soldiers . . . when?" The boy didn't pick up on my agitation, and he continued without hesitation.

"A week ago. She met them right there." He pointed to the gate.

"And they did *feaky-feaky*?" I was losing my grip now. Our squad had been the only Americans in the area the week prior. "That isn't true. That was me, and we just talked, no *feaky-feaky*." The boy scowled, caught in his lie, but persisted, as most people would do in that situation, with the facade.

"No. I saw her with American soldiers. I saw her with you. Americans are liars!"

I stepped forward and closed the gap between us.

"You saying I'm a liar, hajji? *Ishta!* Get the fuck out of here!" I was inches from his face, and even as he backed up, Pearson and Sellers came up to make sure I didn't do anything stupid. The BP station was a bad place to fight—often enough, film crews lurked around corners waiting for the chance to film Americans mistreating the locals. I gave him a shove with the muzzle of my weapon and indicated that I was willing to shoot him.

The boy scurried across the road, tripping over himself as he ran. From four lanes away, he found his tongue and yelled threateningly to me.

"No more Leena! It is dangerous to talk to Americans!"

"That's it, I'm fucking shooting him," I said with only minimal emotion and I raised my weapon. Sellers put a hand on my gun and grabbed my shoulder, calming me down.

"Fuck him, man, fucking dune coon, don't mean nothing."

The moment passed, and I regained my composure. The remainder of the morning went by without any excitement.

It wasn't until lunchtime that we noticed Cum wasn't to be found. We asked Whalee and the local workers, but they had no idea where he was, just that they hadn't seen him that day. For all our distance from the Iraqi people, we had begun to like the kid. Worried about my buddy, I approached Kreed.

"Hey, Sar'nt, Cum isn't around and neither is Leena. Some kid was talking shit earlier, and I think something happened. I know they're just hajjis, but still, you know, its kinda my fault for talking to them." Before long there was a team of soldiers warily creeping up the street to her house. We hugged the walls, keen to the smell of danger and fear that wasn't in the little suburb before. I could hear my equipment creaking beneath its own weight. My boots pounded on the pavement, and sweat beaded into my eyes, making them sting.

When we reached Leena's house, it was as I had feared. The

wall was still intact, but the house itself was razed. A fire had eaten up everything but the sturdiest of foundations. Across the street, one of the neighbors peeked through their gate and I yelled over to her.

"Where's Leena?" The woman didn't answer. She just fearfully slammed her gate and fled into her house.

"Fuck, man. That sucks." Fucking Sellers, but no one had anything else to say. We walked back to the station and went back to work.

# SEVEN

# SHARKS IN THE TIGRIS

S PECIALIST GLEASON yawned loudly, sucking in much of the cool night air. He stretched his arms out above his head and we all heard the sound of Velcro ripping open.

"Fucking body armor is too small," he moaned, struggling to readjust it.

"They don't have any bigger ones?"

"Nope, fucking Sergeant Swain says this is the biggest they got."

"Sucks, man." Washington had heard it all too many times before. Gleason was big, almost too big for his uniform top to even fit, let alone any vest. Before he had left for Iraq, he

bench-pressed over five hundred pounds, and although undoubtedly some of that muscle had turned into fat, he was still
more than an imposing figure.

"Man, this is some boring shit. What time is it?" Washington asked, trying to suppress the yawn he had just caught from
Gleason.

"Around two-thirty. Two hours left."

Pulling duty on the observation posts was universally boring, and any excitement at all was the rarity. Occasionally,
some hajji would drink too much Turkish whiskey and get up
the nerve to shoot at the positions. There was never any real
danger of getting hit from the drunken snipers. "Fuck you,
America!" they would yell up at us with whiskey voices.

Sometimes they would be original and mix things up. "Go
home, America!"

We all thought that was a great idea and that it was heart-
warming that we could agree with the locals on something.
But we didn't go home, not for a while. We just sat there and
looked over the Tigris River into the old city.

We were close enough to throw rocks into the murky water and watch dirty kids swim against its swift current. People
said if you went north, past Baghdad, it was clear like spring-
water, but I never saw it. Where we were it was the hue of day-
old coffee and debris floated so thick you could skip across it
without getting your feet wet.

"You know there used to be bull sharks this far north in the
Tigris?" Sellers told me once. He had just read a book about
man-eaters. "It got too polluted for them to live here. Too bad

there aren't any now. Wouldn't that be some shit? Fucking hajji getting eaten up."

"Yeah, I'd pay a dollar to see that."

"Fuck, man, probably spit out the nasty little bastard." There was no love lost between us and the Iraqis who crowded the riverbanks. Beer and liquor stands would open as nightfall approached. Lanterns and headlights cast an eerie pallor on the makeshift carts. The men would drink openly and profusely, clapping, dancing, and eyeing us with disdain. Their curses could be heard late into the evening, when one by one they would climb into dilapidated clown cars and speed away. The ones who couldn't make it that far simply slept on the riverbank among the trash and homeless kids.

We kept a close and wary watch on them. We had ruled it illegal to drink so close to our compound, but even when it was enforced they never stopped. These Iraqis may have given up their political and national sovereignty, but they held fast to their favorite drinking spot.

River Road, as we had creatively dubbed it, was our convoy route in, and too many IEDs—improvised explosive devices— had already been set on the narrow two-lane road. Specialist Pohl, just back from Afghanistan, had been wounded there a few days before, along with Renfroe and Sergeant Hall. Doc Moss had his eardrums blown out, and Meherwin had lost part of his foot. No one liked traveling down that road. Wise had emptied his brains into his Kevlar helmet on that shit-infested street.

"Kill me, America! I hate you! Shoot me!" Voices slurred by

alcohol and poor English would reach our ears four stories up where we sat, just waiting for something to do.

"SOG, SOG, this is OP One. We got a hajji down here begging us to shoot him, over."

"OP One, this is SOG. Is he armed? Over." They knew that if he were, we would have already dumped him.

"Negative, SOG, over."

"Well, then don't shoot him. SOG out." By then all the other positions would chime in with advice and smart-ass comments.

"OP One, this is OP Four, send him our way, we'll help him out."

"Hey, go home and get a gun! Come back and I'll shoot you! I promise!" we would yell encouragingly. They never understood, though. They just continued to scream until they either tired of hearing their own voices or some passerby scooped them up.

While the occasional sniper fire from across the river did keep us honest, for the most part OP 1 was a dull way to spend the evening. It did allow for a lot of introspective thought, but when your life has turned to complete shit, you don't really want to spend too much time thinking about it. Even the constant pondering about our homecoming had died out. We were never going home.

Alpha Company crossed the berm into Iraq on the morning of the war. We were with First Marine Expeditionary Force, but they went home right after the invasion. We were attached to the 108th Airborne until they, too, left us. Third Infantry Division used us for a while, until their time for pa-

rades and heroism came during the summer. Now we were
stuck with First Armored Division, and still we sat in a city
that seethed around us. Warriors were replaced by occupiers,
peacekeepers, while we slept every night in the dragon's den,
stirred by its fiery breath. We were riding a crest of hatred two
thousand years old in a storm that no one who hasn't experienced it can understand. We knew what an AK-47 bullet
sounds like when it zips unseen by our heads. We had heard
the deafening blast of 155-millimeter rounds exploding near
us. We knew the screams of the wounded and dying, and had
seen the tears of men, of soldiers. I watched as we de-evolved
into animals, and all this time there was a sinking feeling that
we were changing from hunter to hunted.

Through all this, Gleason and Washington sat and looked
mindlessly out over the Tigris River, counting the minutes until they could go downstairs to their cots and sleep, dream
about better times and better places that would never look the
same to them again. The dreams' details faded over time, and
before you knew it, you couldn't remember what your wife's
or child's face looked like. Sight was always the first memory
to go; the others last longer. I couldn't picture her smile anymore, but I could remember the sound of her voice, or conjure
up the smell of her hair or our house. That was what kept us
sane and yet tortured us. We embraced those memories like
drug addicts shivering on a street corner.

On the next building over, one soldier asked the other, "Hey,
what's going on down there?" There was yelling in the street
below. Both men leaned over, their helmets tipping slightly
forward as they scanned the road like giant birds of prey.

A little white four-door car, its quarter panels almost rusted out, idled directly below them. The driver's voice was distressed as he argued with two drunks in traditional Arab robes who leaned imposingly into the driver's window. The exhaust pulsed out a black smog, like some monster's dying breath, as the three men continued berating one another.

The sounds of shots echoed off the buildings as the two men in the street pulled pistols from beneath their traditional robes and fired wildly at the driver.

With a start, the first soldier on the roof raised his rifle, setting his sights on the men. His first shot hit one of the assailants in the top of the head, crumpling him instantly like a sack of water. The other fellow wasn't as lucky. M-16s fire a bullet not much larger than a civilian .22 round, but moving much faster. The second shot nailed the second hajji in the groin. After a quick bunny hop and a cry of surprise, the man dropped and lay writhing on the dirty street. The shocked but unharmed driver sat stonelike in his car, terrified to move, but no more bullets came his way.

The Quick Reaction Force hurriedly raced into the street. The wounded man lay in the fetal position, cradling his bloodied groin. The bullet had hit him on the head of his penis and run down his shaft. After it hit the pelvis, it curved around and exited through his testicle. Slow-talking Gaddis summed it all up in his Southern drawl when he asked, of no one in particular, "How are you supposed to bandage that?" But somehow they did, and the medics came and took him. They did what they could before sending him off to an Iraqi hospital. Later, with grimaces of disgust, two medics stood outside dumping canteens of water onto the soiled stretcher.

"The interpreter said that guy had just gotten married tonight. Ain't that some shit?" one chubby medic said to the other.

"Yeah, well, fucker shouldn't have tried to carjack somebody right outside our compound on his wedding night."

The chubby medic thought about this a second and then continued. "Yeah, but it still sucks, though."

The other nodded in agreement, and when they were done cleaning up they went back to bed for the few remaining hours of darkness, slightly content in the knowledge that for at least one night, someone else was more unhappy than they were.

# EIGHT

# THE THIRD OF JULY

KREED MOVED SLOWLY up the stairwell. Each footstep was heavier than the last, and although his head was tilted forward with eyes half closed in fatigue, his mouth curved upward in a smile. I sat at the top of the stairs, smoking a cigarette and watching him. There were salt stains on my brown T-shirt from the sweat that had accumulated since its last wash, and with an Iraqi bayonet I cleaned the week-old grime from underneath my fingernails. Three stories below the railing that I rested on was the alleyway that ran between our compound and the neighboring houses. On a nearby roof, an old man with a stick was training pigeons. The flock of birds moved as one in response to his whistles, claps, and gestures.

Palm trees in the distance covered up the plumes of smoke from burning vehicles and buildings. It was still early in the day, and the sun had yet to reach its peak.

"What's up, Kreed?" I asked without bothering to look up.

"Wha . . . What, man?" His voice was drawn out and tired.

"I said what's up?"

"Oh, right. Nothing, man. Just chilling, you know." The slur was apparent, and when I glanced over curiously, my eyes found his dull and glazed over.

"Dude, what are you on?" My curiosity was piqued, and I pocketed the knife and dropped off the bannister onto my heels.

"What?" He looked confused as to where he was. There were plenty of blue and white pills around—whatever pharmaceuticals we could get our hands on—but none that gave the results Kreed was showing. I didn't know what it was, but I knew I wanted in.

"Kreed." I took a pause to laugh. "You're all fucked up, bro. What are you on? You gotta hook my ass up, you know?"

Kreed moved in slow motion, first looking left, then right, as if imparting the secrets of the universe. "Man, go down to the aid station. Tell Doc Little that you have the shits and to give you what he gave to the Kreed Dog. Don't tell no one else, though."

"Yeah, no problem. Is he down there now?" I was already putting on my uniform top and reaching for a rifle from the rack we had hung just inside our door.

"Hey, man, I'm gonna chill out for a while, maybe take a

nap later." Kreed's shuffling feet were my prompt that the conversation was over, and before I could get to the stairs I saw him collapsing facedown on his cot.

*Shit, I gotta try this stuff.* My feet were already gliding down the three flights of concrete steps like a child's on Christmas morning.

The compound was never really still, even at night. There were always patrols coming and going, and guard reliefs walked doggedly out to positions as the soldiers they were replacing staggered toward their beds looking equally drained. It had the feel of an old train station, with people constantly passing by and giving greetings, regardless of how crude the wording.

The aid station was at least half a klick from my barracks. That isn't particularly far, but I was sure it had been a hell of a hump for Kreed and whatever drug had walked with him. What's more, I wasn't sure that the medics would be altogether pleased to see me. Kreed had formerly been a part of Headquarters Company, so all the medics knew him well. I had only one or two friends over there, as headquarters and line people don't mesh very well. I had second thoughts about going into the aid station at all, but the idea of escape, if only for a few hours, was too tempting.

Pushing aside a heavy wool blanket that served as a door to the aid station, I was met with a gust of cold air. Their air conditioners were pumping overtime, and I felt a pang of jealousy as I thought of the medics sitting in there all day long, playing video games and flirting with the two nurses we had picked up as translators.

The cots were arranged geometrically in the room, and as I passed the first few empty ones, my eyes fell on the youngest and prettiest of the nurses. I stared longingly and with little subtlety at her flowing hair, oversized breasts, and dark eyes.

"She's something, ain't she?" Doc Little had snuck up on me from behind. We had spoken a few times before, and he had always seemed like a pretty cool guy.

"She's fucking smoking hot. What's her deal?" I asked without taking my eyes off her. She was wearing jeans and a long-sleeved shirt. Her attire, though conservative by American standards, was incredibly seductive to a tired soldier away from home. This goddess of the aid station rested comfortably on a desk, one leg crossed over the other as she dealt with no fewer than three soldiers, crowded around her. She was too busy with them to even notice me standing in the center of the room.

"I don't know. I hear some captain in Headquarters Company is fucking her," Little murmured into my ear.

"Man, ain't it always the same. We do all the work and they get all the pussy. Fucked up."

"You got that shit right, Crawford, same everywhere. So what's up? You sick?"

I always got freaked out in aid stations. It wasn't that I was scared of needles or pain. I had problems with admitting I needed help. Most good light infantrymen tend to ignore their aches and pains. To be seen in the aid station is to admit weakness.

There were already two soldiers laid out on cots, their faces pale and eyes half closed. One rubbed his forehead in pain, while the other could have been mistaken for a corpse had his chest not risen ever so slightly. IVs were stuck in their arms, and cool saline flowed through parched veins. They were undoubtedly heat casualties, a common ailment in a land where temperatures soared into the 130s and above.

"Uh, I got the shits, and Kreed told me that whatever you gave him worked really well. I want some of that," I stammered, looking at the ground. I wasn't nervous about lying to the medic—that came all too easy. I was simply afraid of rejection.

"Sure, take off your top and hop on," Little said in his medical voice as he gestured to an empty cot by slapping it a few times with his open palm. Soon I was horizontal on the high bed, staring up at the triangular designs on the ceiling. My desert uniform top was wrinkled up in my left hand and my boots knocked together impatiently as I waited for him to return.

When Doc Little returned with an IV bag, I was a bit perturbed. As I said, needles have never bothered me, but I would have hated for someone to mistake me for a heat casualty like those other two broken dicks.

Doc hit my vein on the first try, and with a tube hanging out of my arm, I watched as one thousand milliliters of saline slowly poured into my veins. Doc returned with a clipboard and handed it to me along with a pen.

"Sign this and put your social on it," he instructed without any fanfare. When the paperwork was complete, Doc placed it on a small desk and retrieved something from a drawer. He returned to me with a big smile on his face. I suppose it's a good feeling being the guy who can make anyone feel better any-time. In his hand was a small syringe, and there was no ques-tion as to what it was. I tried not to grin like some junkie about to get his fix, but I had never tried morphine and was more than a little excited about it. He injected it straight into the IV bag and then gave me a tap on the arm.

"This ought to help. Let me know when you're ready to go."

"Thanks, Doc."

"No problem." And with that he returned to wherever it is that medics hide out when they don't want to deal with the aches and pains of soldiers.

The fluids from the IV were cold. They kept them refriger-ated in order to lower the core body temperature of heat ca-sualties. I could feel the solution as it passed from vein to vein. Every inch of my body cooled down, one at a time. I turned my head to the side to see if I could still see the young nurse who was lounging erotically on a low table. Every so often she would whisk the hair away from her round face with a shake of her head. She looked over at me and smiled sweetly. I re-turned it with a goofy teenaged grin.

"Oh shit," I mumbled to myself as she slid smoothly off the table and began slinking toward me like a tiger on the prowl. It occurred to me that maybe Western women weren't the only ones who could get what they wanted from a man.

"Allo." Her voice was soft and carried a strong English ac-cent. "Wot's your name?" The melody that came from her mouth was entrancing. My lips were parched, and the sound of my own voice was full of scratch and dirt. Hearing it em-barrassed me, and I kept my answers short.

"Uh, Crawford. John Crawford." I felt like she could see right through me, but if she recognized my discomfort, she didn't acknowledge it with anything other than a smile. Her lips parted in a sweet smile, and she playfully bit her tongue.

"Are you sick? Some dysentery, perhaps?" I was horrified.

"Hell no . . . I mean, well. I didn't feel great and, uhm . . . so . . ." My voice trailed off. I didn't want her to know why I was there, but I sure didn't want her imagining me shitting all over myself, either. She just giggled, and I lost myself in her eyes.

"Well, I hope you feel better. I will see you again, I hope." Her hand touched mine, and I caught my breath. She turned and strode away on those perfect legs, making sure I watched her until even my craning neck couldn't keep her in sight.

"God bless nurses," I whispered in gratitude, and looked back toward the ceiling. The designs on it were becoming blurry, and part of me began to wonder if the conversation had even taken place or if it had been a hallucination. The medics strode by at incredible speed, their voices sounding like an Alvin and the Chipmunks singalong. The vinyl cot stretched underneath me, making little groaning sounds of its own. My face tingled with the cool air that touched it, and there was a slight scent that I couldn't quite place. Not the smell of sickness, like a nursing home, but the clean smell of waiting rooms. Light entered through the fabric covering the window, lending a strange tint to the room that swam with the fluorescent lights in the ceiling.

"Wow, I am really fucked up," I managed to mumble before my eyes closed and the world became dark.

"Hey, Crawford." I could feel something shaking me, grasping my shoulder, but when I struggled, my body didn't respond.

"You ready to go?" Doc Little was there. His face slowly came into focus, though his voice sounded like he was talking underwater.

"What?" My own voice was equally garbled, and I didn't remember where I was.

"I said are you ready to go? You've been here like thirty minutes."

"I have?" I inquired with a thick tongue. I glanced at my wrist, but even when I realized my watch wasn't on I continued to stare at it, waiting for the correct time to appear.

"Sure, man, I'm good to go."

Doc pulled the needle from my arm and taped a small piece of gauze there.

"See ya later, bro," he called to me, but I didn't answer. My feet felt dipped in lead, and walking was proving very difficult. I shuffled past the curtain, and the sun blinded me. Shielding my eyes with one hand, I grabbed a metal railing with the other and steadied myself. I could see my barracks, but they seemed a flickering desert mirage and were certainly an impossible distance. I hesitated to start. What had I gotten myself into? A few feet off of the sidewalk were bushes, and they seemed a great place to rest, if only for a little while.

"Hey, faggot, what's going on?" An omnipotent voice rang out above me, and I put my hands on my head to protect me.

"Hey." The voice wasn't that of God, and I breathed a sigh of relief and slowly turned, nearly toppling. The world was orbiting at warp speed and didn't appreciate my snail's pace.

When I got my balance, I could see Specialist Gaddis standing before me. He was an avid bodybuilder, a biochemistry major, and the slowest talker I have ever met. His drawl sounded like Eeyore from the Winnie-the-Pooh cartoons. It was easy to mistake him for some ignoramus if you didn't listen to the actual words he said rather than the way he said them. Today, though, he sounded normal, and for once it was him who mocked me for speaking slowly.

"What the fuck are you doing?" There was laughter in his tone. He could tell I was fucked up.

"Nothing, man . . ." I tried to remember where I had been going.

"I'm on my way upstairs, man. I'm . . . shit." I gasped for breath; all the thinking had worn me out.

"C'mon, I'll walk you upstairs. You get caught by the first sergeant like this and you're fucked." Gaddis grabbed my arm, and without protest I allowed myself to be led across the sandy lot separating the buildings. It seemed that everyone we passed eyed me suspiciously, and I was sure that any second some high-ranking officer was going to snatch me away and bring me in front of the battalion commander.

Gaddis somehow got me up the stairs and into my room, where, barely conscious, I collapsed onto my cot, sending mushroom clouds of dirt into the air. The last sound I heard before darkness engulfed me was Kreed's snoring.

My ears were the first thing to wake up.

"Dude, we have to. It's Fourth of July, after all."

"I don't know, if we have to go out . . ."

"We won't. We don't have patrols for like thirty-six hours."

Voices pierced the fog around me, and I slowly became aware of my surroundings.

"C'mon, you know it sounds fun." It was Brunelle, and he was arguing something with the others in my squad.

"I don't think it's a good idea, guys. We could get in a lot of trouble."

"But you're the Kreed Dog—you never get in trouble." There was Sellers.

"Shit," I mumbled, wiping the saliva from my open mouth. The lights were off in my room, and their voices were the only thing that pierced the blackness. The room next door was alive with their debate. My joints were filled with superglue, and I groaned when I sat up. I held my head in both hands, trying to get it together. My legs were still shaky, but they did their job, and I slowly shuffled into the land of the living.

"Hey, Crawford's up!"

"Yeah, fuck you, guys," I growled with eyes half shut. I stopped at the mini-fridge that I had acquired from the 101st months before. It was unreliable, but a far cry from drinking scalding water. I opened the door and searched the contents.

"Where's my strawberry milk?" My hands groped through the dark fridge, tipping over water bottles and soda cans. "Who drank my fucking milk?"

"Hey, Kreed, what's that under your bunk?" Sellers asked with his faux-serious voice. Turning to investigate, I caught sight of a small pink cardboard milk container hidden from view by Kreed's guilty boot.

"Aw, man, I saved that from breakfast. Fucking Ali Baba." Kreed looked genuinely ashamed and began to apologize and explain himself. He was a supernice guy; you met him once and really wanted him to like you. He could smooth-talk anyone, and we all said he could be a politician. The fact that he got us out of a lot of stupid shit with that forked tongue more than made up for a few missing strawberry milks.

I snatched up a half-empty water bottle with my initials scrawled on the cap in black Magic Marker. I plopped down on the cot next to Kreed and guzzled as much as I could before my lungs gave in and I was forced to come up choking for air.

"So that settles it. You owe Crawford. Now you have to do it," Whigham chimed in from his perch by the wall. Around him hung, neatly arranged, an assortment of tools, weapons, and knickknacks. He was the type of soldier that was never short on equipment. He had a tool for every possible situation. Specialist Whigham was a cop back in Thomasville, Georgia, and his new bride had just had their first child.

"That settles what?" My head had become clearer, and my eyes focused on the room. Most of the squad was in there, and they all looked toward Kreed, sensing that his resolve was beginning to waver.

"We think, since tomorrow is the Fourth of July, our fine nation's Independence Day, that we should honor it by having a celebration," Whigham replied with mock diplomacy.

"Celebrate?" I ventured a dangerous smile. In my current condition, celebration was about the farthest thing from my mind, but even the hint of any kind of fun around here wasn't to be dismissed.

"These fuckers think we should go steal beer from the hajjis down by the river," Kreed explained.

"Confiscate. Not steal. Confiscate," Sellers corrected. None of us had had much to drink in the preceding months. Occasionally, a bottle of whiskey would find its way into our room. You could buy a bottle of Turkish whiskey in Baghdad for five dollars. But more often than not, we stuck to pills and, well, on that day, morphine.

"And we're mounted on our first patrol, so we can just throw it in the back of the Humvee. No problem," Whigham continued.

"If everyone brought empty assault packs, we could fill them with beer and no one would see us carry them upstairs," I added, finally grasping the plan and embracing it.

"Bingo," someone said.

"If something happens in sector, and we have to go out again—" Kreed began.

"We won't," came the instant rebuttal.

"All I'm saying is that hajji doesn't write our op orders and they don't go by our schedule. Just 'cause we're not supposed to go out doesn't mean we won't have to." We were silent for a second as reason and common sense battled with desperation and boredom. It wasn't a long fight.

"Even if we do get called out, we know this place like our own backyards now." Heads nodded in agreement. "Besides, how drunk can we get on a couple of beers? Just like three or four per person."

Eventually, Kreed turned his back to us and pretended to sleep.

"Shut up, fuckers. I don't want to hear any more." We could already smell the barley and taste the hops.

Someone in higher had decreed that the consumption of alcohol was strictly forbidden on the streets. Regardless, every evening by 1600 hours, beat-up cars would begin lining up along the riverfront behind our compound, their seats full of young Iraqis and their trunks full of beer. I never found a bar in our sector, although there was a liquor store in the northern side of Maghrib. Drinking laws were a technicality in what had been the most secular state in the Middle East prior to the invasion. Every night men would dance about in drunken stupors, the street lit by kerosene lamps placed strategically among carts selling alcohol. The stands sold Turkish and Dutch beer along with cheap whiskey.

Usually, we were content to watch them from above, but on numerous occasions we had been sent down to break up their party like cops harassing spring breakers. Curses and threats would surround us as coolers were dumped, their contents swallowed into the gloomy depths of the Tigris River. It was such a waste, and the outcome was inevitable. Not even the most professional soldier can go to work for twenty-four hours a day, three hundred sixty-five days a year. We were a bomb waiting to go off.

The precedent had been set, so when our Humvee pulled up to the rabble, the partyers moved about nervously. Their revelry hadn't even begun yet. It was still light out, and here we were breaking up the party already. Some moved slowly away, hoping to escape with whatever alcohol they had on them; others stood about looking innocently at us.

Whigham and I had volunteered to take point on this operation. He could easily draw from his police experience confiscating beer from partying teenagers back in America, and me because . . . well, now I really wanted a beer. We tackled this mission with the same professionalism and demeanor we would a raid.

"What's in the trunk?" Whigham would ask as I provided security. When beer was discovered, we would haul it out of the trunk and slide it into the back of a cargo Humvee. We did this quickly and soon had well over a case of Turkish beer—or blue gills, as we called them because of the silver-and-blue designs on the can.

The Iraqis realized that this was no condoned operation, and in an attempt to salvage their evening, they offered us half of the beer. Whigham and I ignored their pleas and took it all. To admit that we were simply stealing their alcohol would have caused us to lose all semblance of moral authority.

Kreed, however, had no such delusions, and as I slid another cooler full of cold beer into the Humvee, I caught sight of him shelling out cash to the would-be drunks. The hajjis smiled, and one offered him an open beer. He obligingly took a sip before handing it back with a baby-kissing smile. He really was a politician.

"Mistah! Mistah! Here." An Iraqi handed an open beer to me. I initially declined, but after some prodding accepted the offer, if only to get the man away from me. One by one, the soldiers around me gave in to the prompts of the Iraqis and took a sip or two of our Fourth of July stash. Sellers was behind me, voraciously downing beer after beer. Finally, we climbed onto our Humvee full of beer and started back home.

"Hey, Crawford, one more beer, c'mon," Sellers pleaded

with me as I loaded beer cans into the empty assault packs that had been cached in the back of the Humvee with me and tossed the empty coolers out the back of our speeding vehicle onto the dingy streets.

"All right, man, I'll share one with you." I didn't know how many Sellers had drunk, but I had only had one full beer, and my head swam from the alcohol and the sun. Beer goggles didn't make Baghdad any prettier a sight, and we were glad to pull through the gate and into the compound.

"Next patrol is on foot in three hours. I'm gonna go fill out the mission data sheet," Kreed yelled to us as we hopped from the vehicles, cans clattering on our backs. While Kreed was in the command post filling out the hopelessly complex paperwork that the army required just to get out of bed in the morning, the temptation back in the room was becoming un-bearable.

It had started with Sellers talking us into having just one more beer. That one turned into two, then four, until soon enough the Fourth of July party was over and all the beer gone. We laughed like schoolboys who had sneaked away with a bottle of their father's bourbon. Pearson and Hightower sat opposite each other and took turns vomiting into a black plastic bag they both held. It was a one-hour drinking frenzy.

Whigham stood precariously, laughing, over Sellers, who had passed out while cradling a mannequin leg he had found and named Kim, after his girlfriend. I ended up in the dingy bathroom connected to our room, curled into the fetal position, my head resting on a rice bag full of laundry detergent.

Then Kreed came back. He had returned to empty beer

cans littered about and a combat-ineffective squad. His tirade was controlled, like that of a father who is more disappointed than angry. Sellers was sitting up, his eyes confused, and any attempt he made in protest was quickly discounted. Kreed turned on me, rage in his eyes.

"Crawford! Are you drunk too, damnit?!"

"What? Naw, I'm cool," I slurred as Kreed shook his head with disgust.

"You two outside!" Kreed motioned to the two team leaders and stormed out of the room. Brunelle and an increasingly clumsy Sellers followed to receive the private scolding that everyone knew was coming. We put off the next patrol a few more hours, and even then we had to leave Sellers behind, still too drunk to function.

There was no soothing oblivion for us that Fourth of July. Kreed took us on a blistering patrol from one end of the sector to the other and back. It was a quiet and stuffy night, with little activity. The silence was broken up only by the sound of soldiers vomiting in the shadows as they walked, and I vaguely remember making a promise never to drink again.

# NINE

# NO CRYING
# IN BASEBALL

THE SATELLITE PHONE was hot against my cheek. It was barely ten A.M. and already the temperature was soaring into the triple digits. "C'mon, answer. Answer." On the fourth mechanical ring, I heard a barely audible "Hello."

"Hey, darling," I said in my sweetest voice, scarcely able to contain my excitement. I had been away from home for eight months, and no matter how many times I called, I always got shivers any time my wife answered the phone.

"Oh, hey." I could hear the tension in her voice. I prepared myself for the worst.

"Is everything okay?" I realized I was holding my breath in

anticipation. When all you have time to do is worry about what is going on at home, you start to imagine some terrible things.

"No." She let out a long dramatic sigh and then continued. "Murphy shit all over the house, ate the cushions on the sofa and a pair of my shoes, and I've only been gone for a couple hours."

I tried unsuccessfully to suppress a smile, sure she could hear it. She had bought that puppy before we were married, and over a year later it was still a monster.

"I'm sorry, hon." I gave her my best sympathetic voice, but I think its insensitivity was detected.

"Fuck, more piss!" Stephanie blurted out and I imagined she stumbled onto another sticky puddle.

"Well, it could be worse. I mean, I'd give anything to be at home cleaning up dog shit."

"What could be grosser than cleaning up a house full of dog shit?" The disgust in her voice was palpable.

"Try cleaning up brains." I tried to catch the words and pull them back even as they left my mouth. It's hard living with a bunch of soldiers and then trying to talk like a normal person to your wife on the phone.

"When did you clean up brains? Tell me about it, I want to know." There was curiosity and naiveté in her voice, but the self-pity was gone. *What can it hurt?* So I told her about my day.

WE HAD BEEN the battalion Quick Reaction Force for three uneventful days, and I was enjoying the time to myself, getting more than a full night's sleep and relaxing.

"Wake up, we gotta go!" Sergeant Brunelle stormed into our room, the door slamming behind him.

"What's going on?" I groaned through half-closed eyes.

"Pohl's squad got hit. Get your shit on." And just as quickly as he had entered, Brunelle turned and left the room, heading back to his own bunk and his gear.

"Shit" was all I could muster, and that about summed it up. It took the squad less than five minutes to get on our gear and get in the Humvees. I looked at my watch; it was four forty-five in the morning.

"You gotta love this job," I joked halfheartedly as we kicked up gravel leaving the back gate. No one responded.

Our destination was right around the corner, and it took only a minute or so to get there. I clambered out of the vehicle, fighting against gravity and sleepiness. There was already a squad there, and in between the hovering soldiers was a smoking BMW, the motor rattling loudly. On the rooftops of the dilapidated apartment buildings around us were underwear-clad Iraqi men watching the show.

"Hey, Pohl, what's going on?" I asked lazily as I sauntered up to the crowd. They parted, and I got my answer.

"We were on our way in and this fucker drives by with his lights off. When he sees us, he hauls ass," Pohl's voice continued, but I could scarcely hear it as I stared at the carnage.

"So we took off after them, and this dick starts shooting at us. So Reeves lit their asses up. Only two shots, can you believe it?" I glanced up at Specialist Reeves, a slight-voiced country boy from south Georgia who looked more like a mechanic than a soldier. He was still struggling with the Browning Mark II fifty-caliber machine gun mounted on top of his Humvee. He had only fired two shots because there was a malfunction and the weapon wouldn't come back up.

On the ground were two blood-soaked Iraqi men. Both were on their faces with their hands tied behind their backs. The skinnier one was crying, and with a nudge of the foot someone tried to shut him up. "There's no crying in baseball." We all giggled a little at that.

The other guy was overweight and had a full head of curly hair. He was so drenched in blood and chunks of meat that I asked repeatedly if he was hit. "I don't think so" was the response. We almost never had an interpreter with us, and I contemplated reaching down and checking him for wounds, but I didn't have any rubber gloves, and there was no way I was getting that shit all over me. He just stared straight ahead with eyes like saucers. Then I turned to the car.

A fifty-caliber round is one hell of a big bullet. Built for destroying light armored vehicles and aircraft, it is not intended to be used on people. Reeves may have fired only two shots, but at closer than fifty meters, his accuracy was never in question. The first round entered at the bumper and went through the trunk. It slammed into the left backseat passenger, the one with the rifle. His hip was blown inside out, and it was impossible to tell where his torso ended and his legs began. They were twisted over each other, and the jagged edges of bones emerged in odd places. The bullet then continued forward, hitting the driver's hand and cutting it in half before finally passing through the speedometer and embedding itself in the engine block.

The machine gun, bucking against the first explosion, sent

the second bullet higher. That one hit the unlucky fellow without the hips on the right side of his head; a chunk the size of my open hand was missing. The bullet then continued, no longer flying straight but tumbling, and impacted in the center of the driver's neck, splitting it wide open in a gash that was easily six by eight inches.

The driver now lay slumped over the seat, his spine hanging out of the wound; the blood had slowed to all but a trickle onto the seat. His left hand still rested on the steering wheel, even in death trying to escape by making one last turn to get their car out of the sector. The gore itself was impressive enough and warranted a moment to notice, but it was what the man in back was doing that had all our hearts in our mouths. He was looking at us, both eyes perfectly focused despite the fact that half his brain was all over the car.

*Just nerves*, I thought. *His nerves are popping and he's already dead, like a snake after you cut off its head.* The analogy made me smile. But then his eyes shifted, first from me, then to Pohl, then back to me. They settled on me and he began to mumble in Arabic, holding my gaze, staring at me from the abyss. I could see halfway through this man's head and he was looking at me, talking to me in an incomprehensible language. His breath was coming in wheezing gasps, and the hole in his head glistened in the streetlight like fairy dust. The entire car was filled with brain fragments and shards of bone. Had that man gotten up that morning and thought, *I might die today?* What was he thinking now as he realized that his life was over? Was he simply saying the obvious, "Oh fuck, I have a hole the size of a softball in my head and I'm dying"?

I couldn't help but wonder if it was something else; if his jumbled words revealed the mysteries of the universe. Slowly, his eyes dimmed and his voice trailed away. The gasps ebbed and his life gave way. When he fell over onto the seat of the car, the rest of his brain became dislodged and slid onto the floor of the car, leaving a slug's trail behind it. The whole squad was standing there looking, unable to speak, and then it started.

"Hey, Crawford, what do you think the last thing that went through his head was?" Sergeant Howell asked me with half a grin on his face. An overweight medic who had tagged along quoted a line from the movie *Boondock Saints*, a barracks favorite. "Hey, buddy, where you goin' . . . Nowhere!"

"Hey, man, we gotta turn off the car." I don't know who said it, but I walked over to the driver's side and leaned in the window. I couldn't reach the keys without sticking my head all the way into the already reeking vehicle.

"Hey, Sellers, you wanna turn off the car or what?" I called out in an attempt to get out of the inevitable.

"Fuck you, I'm not on brain detail." I looked at the inside of the car again and hesitated. The squat medic with the sense of humor saw the dilemma and stepped in to save the day with his latex gloves.

THE IRAQI POLICE are never prompt, so after calling them we sat back, musing over the breakfast we were missing.

"Hey, you think the cooks got off their lazy asses and even made something?"

"Fuck no, probably coffee and T-rat cake."

It would take over two hours for the Iraqi police to arrive and clean up. The sun peeked its way over the horizon, searching for us. For the time being, we were protected from its probing eye by the shade of nearby buildings. Before long the streets were busy with morning traffic and pedestrians, and half the neighborhood had seen the carnage. As they passed by, we motioned them over in small groups to look closer, and when in curiosity they turned to us, we would gesture to the bodies. "No fucking jerry cans!" we would say, alluding to the common Iraqi practice of illegally reselling gasoline out of buckets and jugs. "Fucking Ali Baba, watch out now." Ali Baba is the generic Arabic term for a thief. After that grew old, and it became apparent that we would miss breakfast chow, we settled down with our MREs for a delicious morning meal. I sat on the hood of the BMW and ate country captain chicken while blood pooled underneath the car and trickled downhill.

"Hey, Crawford, you got brains on your boot," Pohl said matter-of-factly in between bites of chocolate-mint pound cake.

"I'll be damned, I sure do," I answered. Attempting to shake it off proved futile. There was a flake of bone attached, and its sharpened edge was lodged firmly into the rubber sole of my boot. I flicked it off with the handle of my MRE spoon and took another bite of processed chicken in sauce.

THERE WAS SILENCE on the other end of the phone, and I didn't know if I should attribute it to the three-second delay that often plagued our phone conversations.

"Hon, are you there?" I asked, mournful that I had shared something of myself from this shithole country.

"Oh my God, I didn't know. That sounds terrible." Stephanie's voice was full of sympathy and longing, but she was right, she didn't know. No one did, and that was what made it worse, and better.

"What are you gonna do when you get back? I mean, are you going to be okay?"

"Oh yeah, I'll be fine, I'm just tired." My voice was full of confidence, and I prayed that I was appeasing her worries, whatever they were. Either way, she wouldn't complain about cleaning up dog shit anymore. I just wanted her to understand, to tell me it was okay. I needed reassurance. It didn't come, and waiting on the line, I shivered unconsciously despite the heat.

# TEN

# WHALEE'S SHOP

THERE REALLY WERE no desirable missions to be had in those days, but that didn't mean some weren't preferred over others. Mostly we were guarding gas stations and running patrols. There were two operating gasoline stations in our sector. I neglect to count the third because one of Bravo Company's very minimal tasks was to look after that one. We called ours the BP and the Amoco, not because either had any affiliation with those brands, but just because it was easier to say "We're going to the BP station" than to explain that we would be going to a certain grid or mention some other acronym.

Neither was in a good part of town, but the BP was more open and the smaller crowds allowed for better security.

The Amoco, on the other hand, was down a narrow, shit-littered alleyway surrounded by dilapidated buildings and people. A day rarely went by when there wasn't a shooting or other incident there.

The relative safety at the BP wasn't what endeared it to us. What we did come to love was a small auto-parts shack located on the property. The tiny one-room shop was just big enough to house a rack with oil, air filters, and cigarettes, and a worn-out sofa piecemealed together from different fabrics. And blowing right on that couch was a mammoth air cooler. Its aluminum frame jutted a full three feet from the tin wall of the stand, and water dripped constantly from an overflow valve in the back. The design is simple: Inside it a whirring fan blows air over water. The temperature inside might only drop to one hundred degrees, but the difference was marked.

The shop owner's name was Whalee; we pronounced it "Wall-Lee." He had been a noncommissioned officer in the Iraqi army years before, during their infamous war with Iran. Despite the fact that he had served in our enemy's army, there was something about his demeanor that made him likable. He was the closest thing we had to a hajji friend. That is to say, we almost considered him to be a real person. In war, that's about the most you can ask for. His faded jeans and polo shirt matched with his deck shoes in a *Miami Vice* sort of tribute. His beard, though short and stubbly, gave a stern countenance that belied his congenial personality.

Because the shop was so small and full of the necessary wares for driving in Iraq, only one soldier could comfortably join Whalee in there at a time. During the long scorching days, we would place the radio next to the sofa and there we would rotate soldiers out one at a time. The flimsy metal walls gave enough of an illusion of safety that we could take off our helmets and relax while sipping a Pepsi.

On the corner of the shelf was a vintage radio from the era before television. Whalee's grandfather had bought it in his own day, and through it we would listen to President Bush on the BBC. Our host would sit next to us on the couch and babble about politics, war, and love. His English was impeccable, and he was never openly unsupportive of us. Pointing to the wall, he would finger the several bullet holes there.

"When America invaded, Iraqi soldiers and police were gone. The looters came and I fought them here." At this point in the story, Whalee would imitate his position facing the window. His arms would cradle an imaginary Kalashnikov, and with wild-eyed enthusiasm he would trace the paths that bullets meant for him had taken.

At first we didn't take to him more than any other local, but he was always persistent about befriending us. Over the months when we had grown thoroughly disgusted with MREs, Whalee, unwilling to let us out of his sight, would with a snap of his fingers and a harsh yell send some loitering kid up to take an order, and within minutes he would return with plastic bags full of kabobs, chicken and rice, or whatever the day's special was. He would refuse all attempts to pay him back. "No. We are friends. You protect me and Iraq, and I protect you. It is dangerous for you here. I will get you food." Eventually we bought a cooler to sit in his store. Together we would throw in on ice and soda.

One particularly hot afternoon, Sellers and I were standing, bored as always, near the entrance to Whalee's shop. Traffic was very light, and it had the look of a long day. Across the street, on the third floor of a dilapidated apartment building, two young women were waving at us. We waved back, smiling and beckoning them to come down. The women blushed purposefully and hid their faces behind long lines of clothing hung all about the crumbling brown balconies.

"Come down, baby, I'll treat you right," we called out in hopeful voices. But of course they never moved; most women rarely did unless they were prostitutes, and even then only when no one was looking. But these two women eventually started gesturing us to come see them. On most days we would have immediately laughed that off, but there really was no one on the streets, and there hadn't been for days. The rest of the squad could handle security.

"Hey, man, whaddaya think?" Sellers asked.

"Fuck it. Let's do it." We crossed the four lanes dividing the BP and their apartment. Moving carefully, with weapons at the ready, we sloshed through a pile of backed-up sewage and crept next to the stairway that led up to their room. We had all been in the building before numerous times, as the roof had a locking door and made a good sniper position. Slowly and cautiously, we climbed up the stairs. When we came to the hallway, we crept catlike down it, our weapons in our shoulders, their barrels eyeing every nook and cranny.

The door at the end was open, and I could see some sixties green furniture and the backlight of an old television with rabbit ears blasting static against an infuriated mirror. The two girls, who were in their mid-twenties, came to the door with a rush of giggling and embarrassment. Still we moved slow. Sellers and I eased up next to the door, and I stacked behind him as he defiantly stuck his barrel and head around the corner. The sound of an angry woman met him, followed promptly by a door slammed in his face. We turned and made our way back down the stairs, through the shit creek, and across the street.

After a few minutes of laughter, we calmed down and I noticed that a young Iraqi boy was waiting quietly for an opening.

"John, Whalee." His English was atrocious, but from his pointing at me and Sellers, then back to Whalee's shop, we got the idea that Whalee wanted to see us. We eyed each other nervously, shifting our weight from leg to leg.

"You go in, man, he likes you more." Sellers said to me with the look of a kid waiting outside the dean's office.

"Fuck that, you outrank me."

"Good, in that case . . . you go in." He had me there. I walked into the shop, unsure of what awaited me.

"What's up, Whalee?" I threw out in my best "I'm the occupier of your country" voice.

"Friend, you want girls, I will get you girls, you want food or beera, I will get it. You don't go across the street alone."

"C'mon." I smiled, hoping to change his stern countenance. "I was with Sellers, we just crossed the street real fast, there were some girls smiling at us. We were just playing."

"This is no place to play, people will kill you, it is dangerous. I told you, you want girls, I will get you girls. Otherwise, stay where I can take care of you." Whalee stared me directly in the eyes, unconcerned that in front of him stood an American soldier in full battle rattle carrying a machine gun. I realized I was already feeling like a six-year-old, so I offered a meek "Sorry, we'll be more careful" and scurried out.

A FEW WEEKS LATER, another particularly hot day, and now it was me slumped on the sofa, allowing the cool air to blow directly into my face, my helmet on my lap and my squad automatic weapon on its bipod legs at my feet. A middle-aged Iraqi and his young son came into the store and started talking to Whalee. I had eyed the man briefly upon his entrance and concluded that he was not a threat. Cigarette dangling from my lips, I reached into my pocket for a lighter. When I glanced back up, the unobtrusive man's arm was stretched out to his front and in his hand was a chrome-covered nine-millimeter Taurus, its hammer cocked, the muzzle inches from my nose.

The sounds of the BBC were drowned out by a whirring in my ears. I was done. I glanced down at my weapon lying next to me where I had imagined I would be able to get to it quickly. Useless. It was over. The guy would never get away, of course, there were other soldiers right outside the door. He would die as quickly and violently as I would, but that was little comfort. His eyes were cold and calm. Whalee's eyes were huge with fear, and I could see him searching for his voice.

Realizing that I was dead came with a certain comfort. Nothing I did could possibly fuck up the situation any more

than it already was. With my left hand I grasped the rim of my
helmet—if I moved fast enough, I might be able to knock the
gun away and then drop him with a helmet to the side of his
head. Even as I tensed to move, I saw his finger squeeze on the
trigger and a bright orange flame flash out of the barrel.

Nothing happened. I didn't see my life flash before my
eyes, or even a bright light at the end of a tunnel. What I saw
was a laughing Iraqi man holding a cigarette lighter made to
look like a pistol. He leaned forward to light my cigarette, a
gleam in his eye at the joke he had just played.

Before I could administer the beating that I felt this man so
deserved, Whalee pounced. He snatched the lighter out of the
man's hand and proceeded to belt him on the back of the head
with it. Whalee chased him across the parking lot, raining blows
to the man's back and head while he fled, his child in tow.

Whalee returned victorious but out of breath. After a moment, he began to laugh uncontrollably. After a moment, I too
smiled, though my cigarette shook in my fingers, spilling ash
onto the already dusty floor.


WHALEE'S BROTHER WAS equally likable. His short-cropped
hair and square jaw had immediately reminded me of my un-
cle Jeff in Florida. He didn't speak any English, though, and
Whalee was forced to translate for him.

"How did his arm get broken?" I asked one day, mindful of
the sling that had held his brother's right arm since the day I
met him.

"We have a brother in Jordan," he told me, pausing as if that were an answer, casting a glance at his brother. When he continued, he spoke quickly. "My brother went to visit him, and when he reached the border, the Iraqi soldiers there said his papers were wrong. They arrested him. He was put in a tiny box in the sun. They fed him old bread and dirty water. Sometimes they would attach electrical wires to here, and here." Whalee gestured to his genitals and then to his head. "Other times they would hang him with chains by his arms. That's why he is in a cast." The brother smiled and offered me another cigarette.

"How did he get out?" I murmured.

"One day they just let him out. Maybe they found out he had nothing to tell them. Who knows? Saddam is crazy."


WHALEE WAS there through most of our time in Baghdad. We brought him pornography and he would slip us whiskey; it was a mutually beneficial relationship. We each had what the other wanted. We had some hint of a Western lifestyle, and he had the closest thing to normalcy that we could find.

Because of rotating schedules, not every soldier in the company got to know him. While we were out patrolling the north sector, an American in our company told him to come out of the store. Angry that he was being treated like a run-of-the-mill Iraqi, Whalee refused. After a heated argument, his head was crashed through the same window that he had once shot looters from. Without Whalee, the BP was no longer the place to be, and shortly thereafter we no longer manned it at all.

# ELEVEN

# WHAT HAPPENS WHEN WAR HAPPENS

I HAD A FRIEND named Robert Wise. He was a good kid, only about twenty-one or so. I had known him back home for a few years before the war. After the World Trade Center was attacked, I was put on guard in Tallahassee. It was a cake job, ten hours of guarding at night. Three days on, one day off. I got orders to get me out of going to classes, and I got paid full active-duty pay. Good money for a starving college student.

Wise was most often on night shift with me. He would bring in his PlayStation and we would sit inside a large army tent and play video games all night. Sometimes we would watch cheesy sci-fi movies. He was a big fan. We would talk about girls and the army, of course. He had a zeal for military life that was surprising for a National Guardsman. He didn't bitch or talk bad about anyone, and I remember he had an awesome score on the physical fitness test. But that's not what I see when I think about him. Whenever anyone asks, all I can remember about him is what he looked like, eyes closed, blood on his face, as we waited for the medevac. Meherwin was screaming, but I can't hear him anymore. People were talking to Wise too.

"It's okay, buddy. You're fine. You're gonna be okay." But I heard them only for a while. Now it's just the sound of rotor blades spinning on a Black Hawk helicopter, of gravel and dust hitting my face in the resulting windstorm. I leaned over, covering Wise's head, and I could smell the sweat and blood and feel the heat of his body. I wanted him to open his eyes—not to smile, just open them and show he was alive—but he wouldn't do it.

People say you leave home, go to war, and become a man. I want to be a little boy again. I want to trust people and not look behind my back.

While I was there I didn't see it the same way, though. I only wanted to punish people for what was happening to me. I wanted to go to my home and my wife, but I didn't have either a home or a wife anymore. Twenty-five years old and nothing to live for. I sat in the tiny bathroom in our barracks. The walls were sixties green and the floor was a chipped and stained brown tile. The toilet was covered in rust. I still don't know how a toilet can rust, but I saw it with my own eyes. And I sat there thinking long and hard. How easy to put a muzzle in your mouth and just fire like Private Pyle did. I was too afraid to do it. I wanted to believe that when I got to America things would be all right. I was wrong; you can never go back home.

I went to the gas station yesterday to buy some cigarettes. An Arabic man was working behind the counter. He turned when he heard the door chime and gave me a broad smile. I walked out. I never wanted to hate anyone; it just sort of happens that way in a war.

# TWELVE

# THE RIDE

I T IS INEVITABLE that at some point life will become drab and dark. It's at these times that we must remember that we are not dead, and there is no better way to prove life to yourself than by doing something incredibly stupid. Those moments are the only ones that you will remember years later. They give experience and build character. The same is true in war, and anytime I tell someone about Iraq, I invariably bring up Steven Mitchell.

Mitchell was what one would affectionately refer to as an independent thinker, and his antics at the very least gave a source of comic relief. Back at Florida State University he was a frat boy, popular with the girls, and good at math. In Iraq he was a constant headache for the chain of command. It was no wonder that we got along so well. He bunked with Kerr, Mears, and Harris, and at night if we weren't on patrol, I would go to their squad room and watch pirated copies of the latest movies. Kerr would drink watered-down Turkish whiskey, while I would down half a dozen Valium and embrace the faux emotions that the drug would bring out.

It became odd for people to see one of us without the other; we even went on each other's patrols whenever time permitted. More often than not, Mitchell would join Second Squad for a brisk walk through the city. My squad was much more compromising and enjoyable than his own Weapons Squad. They had been ambushed and taken casualties early on in the occupation, and that weighed heavily on their minds. No one liked dealing with them, because they were simply too cautious.

Kreed was my squad leader by this time, and although it is rather hard to make a combat patrol in 130-degree heat enjoyable, we did our best. Oftentimes it involved playfully teasing the residents of the city, much as they did to us. Before long, we began to be known among the other squads as goof-offs, but there was never any doubt as to our competence. Whenever missions came down, we were relied upon heavily for breaching and entry. It was a good combination that we had going; the mischievousness kept us all in good spirits and raised morale.

Once again, our job was simple: Keep the peace and preserve order. At one of the local gas stations, the one we called the Amoco, the lines crept around corners for miles, and frustrated Iraqis sat in their cars waiting under the scorching sun for days just to fill up their gas tank. We were the only available targets for the resentment over the lack of fuel nearly a year after the war was declared over. We were all sitting in the most oil-rich country in the world, and even when people could get gas, it was overpriced fuel trucked in by Halliburton from Kuwait and Saudi Arabia. The whole thing was a joke, but it directly affected our lives on a minute-by-minute basis.

As is the case in every war, we were nearly always shorthanded, and it took a lot of manpower to secure the station twenty-four hours a day. To remain efficient, we began running a team of four soldiers and their squad leader at the Amoco at a time, with Kreed staying there all night.

The Amoco was small by American standards. It had six pumps and a small station house dividing them. The four-lane highway known as Delta Road ran directly in front of it, and its lanes were constantly clogged with traffic trying to cut into the station. Civilians crowded the area, accosting us with items for sale, questions, and complaints about the situation.

The Iraqi people had lived for years under an oppressive government, and they had no qualms about being shady to get what they wanted or needed. There were enough shops and homes in the immediate area that drivers would park their cars in front of a shop. They'd get out and wave, explain that it was their home, and then wander inside. The problem wasn't in figuring out if they were telling the truth, because they were always lying. The trick was to catch·them in the act. There was enough money involved in the lucrative business of scalping gasoline to warrant their trouble.

The long hours of leaning against walls staring at people and cars would have been uncomfortable for anyone. Add in a hundred pounds of gear and breathe in nothing but gasoline-spoiled air, and a sense of discontent comes very quickly. To distract ourselves, we would play games with the local children who fawned over us. We would encourage them to wrestle or race on their pieced-together bicycles. The winner would get our praise but little else. We had long stopped giving away food or candy for such trivialities.

On one balmy evening, I found myself short on entertaining children. Mitchell and I leaned against a low barrier watching the passing cars and bustling crowds. I puffed on cheap cigarettes while he talked about a new investment scheme he had conjured up. Then he saw it.

Parked up against the curb was an old rust-red motorcycle with a sidecar. I was surprised that the wheels were still on, but to Mitchell it might as well have been a shiny new wagon, because he was instantly overcome with excitement.

"C'mon, man, let's go check it out." I flicked my cigarette into a puddle of sewage and sauntered over to the bike with him.

"No benzene! No skipping! You wait in line like everyone else!" I barked at the driver, indicating with one hand where the line began. The driver stood next to it on the curb, smiling.

"Mistah, no," was all he could answer. He waved his right hand in a shaking motion at shoulder level. It was the Iraqi gesture for "What the fuck are you talking about?" and was most often accompanied by a confused shaking of the head. He gestured toward a nearby shop, and the implications were clear. He wasn't there for gas, but to visit the shop. Satisfied, I ignored the man's further explanations. The bike was pockmarked with great holes where the metal had succumbed to years of rust. Shaking my head, I couldn't help but mutter, "What a piece of shit."

"Crawford, get in the sidecar." Mitchell's voice was shaky, and I knew that meant trouble. With a laugh, I looked up at him and saw he was serious.

"What the fuck for?" I asked.

"Dude, I wanna drive this thing," he answered as he handled the throttle.

"Bitch, I'm not getting in this shit with you. It probably won't even start. Besides, you can't even drive a bike."

"It's not hard." Mitchell's answer did nothing to ease my trepidation, but I really saw no harm in it. There wasn't much of a crowd that night, and assuming he could even get it running, a quick circle of the gas pumps would be fun enough. No big deal. I stepped inside. My foot immediately began to break through the remnants of the rusty floor, and I had to ease up the pressure I placed on it. Mitchell straddled the seat and attempted to put it into gear, and of course it immediately stalled. The Iraqis who had gathered to watch the show were all but collapsing with laughter. With a shake of my head, I began to climb out of the decrepit hulk of metal.

"Man, hold on a second, I can do this." The urgency in his voice sat me back down again. Sometimes men need a certain normalcy in their lives to remain sane, and I think this was one of those moments for Mitchell. We had gone almost a year without so much as a day off or any real relaxation or fun. Who was I to tell some twenty-one-year-old kid that he couldn't get a laugh out of riding a motorcycle around the parking lot for five minutes?

"All right, fuck it, let's see what you can do."

"Watch this shit, man." A cloud of black smoke rose, and with that the engine began to buck. With a great jerk, we were rolling forward through the parking lot at nearly five miles an hour. Mitchell whooped with joy, his weapon clanging metallically against his body armor. His childlike excitement had me cackling, and all the nearby Iraqis clapped and jumped. They loved to watch us whenever we acted like Americans. From barbaric to decadent without even touching on civilization was how Oscar Wilde had described us, and it was what everyone expected.

The bike continued along straight, and my smile began to fade.

"All right, man, go ahead and turn. . . . Bro, you better turn. Where the fuck are we going?!" My amusement had turned to panic as he hit Delta Road and increased speed simply to avoid being run down by the speeding traffic. It was close to ten at night, and aside from the other three soldiers back at the station, we were the only Americans out at the moment.

"Mitchell, turn the fuck around! Now!" I contemplated leaving his ass and just bailing, but we were already going too fast, and in the middle of traffic.

"I can't turn! It's all fucked up!" Mitchell's smile was gone now too. I pulled my machine gun up out of my lap and placed the bipod legs down on the metallic hood of the sidecar. Two American soldiers cruising down an Iraqi street alone are quite a target, and that was exactly how I felt.

"Stop!"

"I can't! The brakes don't fucking work! Fucking piece of shit."

"Yeah, that's what I said in the first place!"

"Maybe we can do a U-turn up by Delta One!" We had to scream to be heard over the motorcycle's engine, and we both knew that the farther we went, the deeper the shit we were in. "Fuck, that's too far. Turn at Stadium Road!" Things were in full swing, and I was sure that I would die for doing the dumbest thing anyone had ever done. The people we passed were no longer smiling or just watching. They yelled obscenities, and a few threw trash and rocks. As we neared the soccer stadium, Mitchell downshifted and the bike slowed, causing the traffic to loom behind us. I had half a mind to get out and double-time back, but it was far enough that I realized that wasn't much of an option either. The engine began to buck angrily.

"Don't you fucking stall, man!" was all my voice allowed me to say, and it was more of a beg than a command.

"The fucking thing is stuck in third gear, man, there's nothing I can do." As soon as we turned onto Stadium Road, darkness engulfed us. There were no streetlamps or shops, no other cars on the road, only a high wall on the right, and on the left windows and rooftops of Iraqi houses loomed over us like vultures. More than one shot had been fired at us from those darkened portals in the past, and I kept waiting for a bullet to shatter the night as the seconds passed. People appeared out of the dark like wraiths reaching out at us. Their eyes were wet with hatred, and I found myself repeating over and over, "Don't fucking stall. . . . Don't fucking stall. . . . Please don't stall."

Our compound was ahead of us. Any comfort that might have provided me was immediately erased when I realized that anyone on guard would see only a motorcycle with two armed men in it. They wouldn't hesitate to fire. Neither would I were I in their shoes. I was hoping that whoever was on Observation Post 2 was looking elsewhere; American bullets hurt just as bad as Iraqi ones. I was hoping to make a loop and head back to the Amoco.

As we rounded the far corner of the stadium, my hopes actually began to rise. We were now more than two kilometers from the Amoco, but at least we were heading in the right direction. And just as I should have expected, the engine began to sputter and kick at the farthest possible point from safety.

"What the fuck, man? Don't stop here!" I yelled louder, and I could hear the panic in my own voice.

"It's out of gas! Holy shit!" Of course it was out of gas; the man had parked his motorcycle to skip in front of the gas lines. With one last sputter, the engine died and we slowed to a crawl, then stopped completely.

I immediately jumped out and backed into a corner, the stadium to my back and a great pile of debris to my front. I faced out with my weapon at the ready. Mitchell stayed on the bike, trying frantically to start it again. He tugged on the throttle and kicked away, but to no avail. From the consuming gloom phantoms began to appear. They feigned friendly voices, but the sarcasm was hard to miss even in their broken English.

"Mistah, out of benzene?" Angry laughter flittered out of shadows as more and more bearded faces appeared.

"Mitchell, we gotta go!" I yelled, but he continued to fiddle with the motorcycle.

"Hold on, I think we got it."

The faces and voices grew closer. "Mitchell! We gotta go NOW!"

This time, my voice made him turn around, and he looked around and saw what I was seeing. It was the start of a CNN headline: *Two American soldiers were dragged through the streets yesterday after what seemed to be an act of utter stupidity on their part.* Mitchell jumped from the bike and shouldered his weapon. My radio beeped.

"Porn Star, this is Kreed Dog. What is your location, over?" I could barely hear him over the static, and I knew he would hear about the same from my transmission.

"Kreed Dog, this is Porn Star. You don't want to know our current location. We are moving to you, out." I was still hoping to get out of this without too much trouble.

"Mitchell, we're gonna have to run for it." As yet, we hadn't seen any weapons, but that could change instantly.

"All right, give me your weapon, you won't be able to keep up with all that shit." He was right. I was carrying close to nine hundred rounds of 5.56 millimeters and my squad automatic weapon, while he had only his rifle and about two hundred rounds. Hastily, we traded weapons, and with a nod we were off. Like running backs breaking through an offensive line, we raced through the crowd, all the while screaming like banshees, more out of fear than in the hopes that it would make them hesitate. Whatever we did, it worked, and in an instant we were past them.

Once we had running room, we increased our pace to a sprint, or as close to a sprint as one can do when carrying a hundred pounds of equipment and wearing boots. Voices yelled in protest behind us, and the occasional rock stung our legs or bounced off our armored torsos. Still, we increased the pace until pain raked from my side and my breath came in gasps. I glanced back to see that the crowd had given up the chase and a few looters were already pushing the motorcycle away. Past houses and cars and bewildered Iraqis we ran, trying to watch the rooftops, windows, doorways, crowds, and our backs as we went.

Everywhere I looked, wild eyes glared at me and threatened violence. My radio crackled again.

"Porn Star, Kreed Dog, where the fuck are you guys? Over."

"Kreed Dog, Porn Star, gasp, we are, gasp, en route, gasp. Will be there in ten mikes. Out." I could only imagine Kreed's face lined with anger and worry. I was sure he could tell that I was running and out of breath, and yet I was still ten minutes away. I knew we were in for it when we got back, and since I was supposedly the responsible one, I also knew that the blame would end up on my shoulders. Our feet pounded on the pavement, sending splashes of shit water all over us. At times it got almost knee deep, but there was no time to bypass it.

Finally, the faint lights of the Amoco came into view and pierced the darkness. Our pace quickened even as I breathed a sigh of relief. In a moment we were back in our tiny perimeter, hands on our knees, coughing and trying to catch our breath. The sweat from the stress and exertion poured down our relieved faces. After a moment, the owner of the motorcycle came up.

"Mistah?" was all he said with that trademark shaking of his hand and head in bewilderment. Between breaths I managed to point back in the direction of the stadium.

"Ali Baba" was all I could get out, and with a start, the man took off back in the direction we had come from in the hopes of getting back his motorcycle. I looked at Mitchell, and when we made eye contact, neither of us could suppress the laughter that followed. It was real laughter, the kind that comes only when you're making fun of yourself.

A kid walked by selling kabobs, and I bought a bag of them for a dollar. The concoction of goat, peppers, and God knows what else wrapped up in flat bread would make a decent peace offering. With my head down and my breath still coming in gasps, I walked up to a seated Kreed and held them out.

"Hey, we just went to get you something to eat," I said with a guilty smile that I hoped would convince him that we had only been pulling some stupid prank. Kreed didn't even reach out his hand for them.

"C'mon, you know you're hungry, big guy." Kreed finally reached out and took them from my shaking hand, but when I looked at his face, there was no smile.

"Where the fuck have you been?"

"Well, Sar'nt, Mitchell said he could drive this motorcycle, so—" Kreed didn't let me finish.

"Just go away, Crawford."

With a sigh, I turned to walk away, then stopped.

"Yeah, it was stupid, and we could've died. I know that, but it's fucking funny and you know it."

Kreed didn't answer, but I thought I detected a wry grin. He never said anything about it later, and we pretended that it never happened. The rest of the squad knew from monitoring the radio, of course, and they never ceased to tease us about it, nor did the Iraqis at the gas station who saw us drive out and then run back in. For the rest of the year, whenever they saw me or Mitchell they would pretend to throttle a motorcycle and yell out, "Mistah! Vroom-vroom!"

*Naturally, the common people don't want war, but after all, it is the leaders of the country who determine the policy, and it is always a simple matter to drag the people along, whether it is a democracy, or a fascist dictatorship, or a parliament, or a communist dictatorship. Voice or no voice, the people can always be brought to the bidding of the leaders. This is easy. All you have to do is tell them they are being attacked, and denounce the pacifists for lack of patriotism and exposing the country to danger. It works the same in every country.*

—HERMANN GOERING, SPEAKING AT
THE NUREMBERG TRIALS
AFTER WORLD WAR II

# THIRTEEN

# LIES

Y OU GLAD TO BE BACK?" The question was dripping in sarcasm, and though it was too dark to see his face, I knew a
smile was on it.

I answered with a long, drawn-out "Sshhhiiitt."

"Well, man, I don't know. I figured now that you had a
break and all, you be like ready to do this shit. Get it over
with, you know." Sellers was jealous, and I couldn't blame him.
I had just returned from two weeks of leave in America, and it
was my first night back on duty. The city smelled familiar, with
its plumes of smoke hidden in the darkness. Much more familiar than America had.

The two of us were sitting at OP 2, and had been for about thirty minutes before Sellers had spoken. He slumped back in a small canvas folding chair next to me. We would sit in the same kind of seats back at Florida State, tailgating for football games. His body armor and Kevlar were heaped against the lip of the building at his feet, and he bided his time by spitting puddles of Skoal onto the dusty roof.

The wire-framed chair I sat in wasn't nearly as comfortable. After the briefest of moments, it began to dig into your legs and send them to sleep. My Kevlar was on the table in front of me, next to the 240 machine gun that stayed at this position. Links of rounds draped out of it and swirled once in a loop before pouring into a green metal box marked "7.62 linked."

In one hand, a cup of coffee was chilled by the night wind, while in the other was a burning cigarette. The rotations on the roof were long and dull, and it was no oddity for a soldier to smoke an entire pack or dip a can of snuff in one sitting.

"Fuck, man, I think going home made it worse," I said in between puffs of smoke.

"Whatever. I'd do anything to go home. You think now that Mitchell fucked up they'll put me on the list?"

"Shit, they hate you about as much as him. No way you're going home. Anyway, you don't want to. Believe me. Nothing's the same." The commander had picked who would go on leave by a drawing, but it was no surprise when soldiers who weren't favored by the chain of command were skipped over.

"You know I got on the plane to come back to Iraq on my first wedding anniversary?" I continued, looking out.

"No shit, man? Well, at least you were there for part of it, got to see your wife and all."

"Yeah, I guess. You know a reporter asked her how that made her feel? Me leaving on our anniversary? Can you believe that cunt? Fuck, it was harder to leave home this time. I almost didn't come back."

"Shit, man, I wouldn't if it had been me. You'd never see my ass again." Sellers spit again on the roof as if to emphasize his disgust.

We were both full of it. I never considered not coming back, and neither would he. We were still volunteers of a sort, and no matter how shitty things got, I couldn't justify deserting.

"Talk to Kim lately?" I asked, hoping to change the subject.

"Naw, haven't called her in a few weeks."

The silence that followed was profound, and Sellers spit again. It was a quiet night, and because the curfew wasn't being enforced anymore, the occasional car would light up the streets as it flew by. It was cold out this time of year, and all the locals were boarded up in their homes. Slivers of light escaped through cracks under doors and in walls. For a moment I was jealous. Would I trade with them if my family had been somewhere down among the shanties? In that moment, I would be just fine with living in a hovel as long as someone who loved me was there. That's better than the nicest house in northern Virginia any day.

"Well, why haven't you called her?" I finally asked, and after another silence, Sellers answered, his voice slowed by the handful of pills he had taken earlier.

"It was just fucked up. Every time we talked, I was just complaining about things here, and I think she got tired of my bitching. We haven't really had a good conversation in a while. . . . Shit, man, I don't know what's up."

As little as he had said, it was thick with desperation that I'm sure he didn't mean to show. When I had first met Sellers, he had been head over heels for this woman. At night he slept with the old pitted mannequin leg he had named after her. He was always a little off, but there was no doubt that he dug that chick.

The two of us had spent way too many nights like this one, and I had started to feel like I knew Kim about as well as I knew my own wife—as well as anyone really knows anyone, I guess. The despondency was more troubling because I knew exactly what he was going through. We didn't talk about it directly, no one did, but everyone was aware of each other's business. Eyes and ears picked up details, and rumors encapsulated us all—who was getting divorced, whose wife had run off with their kids. All our relationships back home had met their thresholds and broken. We had been away from home for only ten months. So much for true love.

"So what was home like, anyway? I can barely fucking remember it." Sellers glanced over at me as he asked, and I stalled for a moment by lighting another cigarette.

"America was fucking awesome, bro. All the cars were brand new, and trees all over the place, and so many girls you couldn't believe someone ever talked you into leaving in the first place. And the freedom was the best; you could up and go to the gas station or wherever anytime you wanted."

I didn't tell him that being alone, with no one to watch

your back, left you feeling naked and helpless. I spent most of my time watching the rooftops and side roads, looking into my rearview mirror to make sure no one was creeping up on my car from behind. I didn't mention that every Arabic-looking person I saw gave me a funny feeling of anger inside, and that every time I saw someone sitting contentedly inside a coffee shop or restaurant, I wanted to yell at them, wake them up.

"You know my wife and I went to some army post near our house, right? We went to the PX there to see if they had cheaper refrigerators than in DC. They had active-duty soldiers stationed at the gates, and this really fat fuck comes up to me, leans in the window, and wants to see both our IDs, and he's not even polite about it. So I hand them to him, and he says that the decal station is closed and I have to come back the following Monday. So I tell him that I'm back from Iraq on leave and I won't be there long enough to come back. This fat fuck tells me, too bad, that I need to turn the car around and leave. And the whole time his weapon is slung across his back, no magazine in it, and his hands are in his pockets—fucking disgrace, right? They finally let me in, but I had to argue with the NCOIC. I couldn't help thinking that if I could manage to get that fat bastard in my trunk and deliver him hog-tied and duct-taped to the airport, that he should have to take my place here. I think it's a fair deal, like you don't have to come back if you can get someone to take your spot."

Sellers laughed at my story. We all wanted to be heroes when we got back. There was this illusion that none of us would ever have to buy a drink again, that everyone would treat us differently. The only ones excited to see me get off the plane were the reporters. They swarmed in like angry bees. "Are you happy to be home? Did you miss your family?" Of course I fucking did—now get out of the goddamned way. The families themselves—some were so desperate to greet their husbands, sons, and fathers that they would hurl themselves through the crowd of reporters. Others hung back, unsure of how to react to a stranger who looked so familiar.

"When I was a kid, I went to camp, and I remember some of the other kids crying at night and bawling that they wanted to go home. I hated that pussy shit, but man, I wanna go home. I don't know how much longer I can do this. That shit broke me, going home and then leaving again. It's better just to stay here."

Sellers thought about my words for a second or two. "Man, fuck that, I don't care. I'd give anything for leave."

I knew that all over Iraq there were a hundred forty thousand other poor fuckers who were saying the same thing. I dug out another crumpled Iraqi cigarette, losing half the tobacco before I lit it. I hoped a sniper was watching.

"I just don't fucking care anymore, and I don't know what to do," I said under my breath, more to myself than to my friend, but he heard and responded just the same.

"I heard that, man. All you can do is just keep on keeping on. I mean, I'm sure Kim and I will work things out, it's just that things are weird right now." Hearing the confidence in his voice, I couldn't help but feel disgust at how wrong it all was. Nothing was gonna work out—not for him, not for any of us. Our lives were crumbling so that we could pretend to help people who pretended to appreciate it.

"Everything cool with your wife and shit?"

"Yeah, she's great." I put out my cigarette and lit another one, sucking in a deep breath of poison, holding it, then letting it go. I couldn't and wouldn't tell him what was really going on. None of us talked about stuff like that. And as Baghdad slept beneath me, I tried to believe my own lies.

# FOURTEEN

# CHRISTMAS

THERE WERE NO CHRISTMAS carols that year, and no one seemed to miss them. Here and there, stockings could be found stuffed into boxes under someone's cot, their contents ravaged for only the desirable candy and the occasional yo-yo. The weather, while not oppressively hot, was still well into the nineties during the daytime, and it rained at least once a week. Winter storms in the desert sent sand invading the city by night, blinding our patrols.

Sergeant Golder dressed as Santa because none of the other soldiers wanted to, although his costume consisted of little more than a red and white hat and a fake beard. The platoon exchanged gifts begrudgingly. No one was in much of a giving mood. The presents were cans of Copenhagen and green scratch pads for cleaning rusty machine guns. Mitchell put on brown thermal underwear, a Rudolph nose, and a set of antlers. Most of us sat sullenly in the corner wishing for the ghost of Christmas past to come to the rescue. We all got thirty minutes of free phone time that night, and the line was long and impatient. Too many times there were no answers on the other end of the line, and disappointed fathers and husbands strayed into quiet corners so that their eyes didn't betray their darkness to others.

The more everyone tried to make it feel like home, the less it did. Officers began to worry about morale, depression, and their own manifest destiny.

"Keep 'em busy," they must've said to each other behind closed doors, and busy we became. That night we went out to execute a TCP, or traffic control point. The entire battalion was involved. Alpha Company spent our time with several of the Iraqi Civil Defense Corps that we had trained over on the intersection of Alpha Two, a monstrous roundabout that connected four different highways. In the center was a massive statue of some long-dead Persian warrior on horseback, a morose reminder of better times.

The night was cold, as all desert nights are, and soon soldiers stood shivering, their neck gaiters pulled up over their ears in an attempt to turn back the icy wind. Every third car would be checked for weapons, bombs, criminals, all of the above. The traffic stretched out in every direction, and the only Christmas lights that night in the city were from the occasional tracer that would arc across the sky in a green and red laser show.

Cold and miserable as we were, comfort was found in torturing the poor souls whom we came across.

"Good evening, *salaam alaikum*," we would say to the cars as they passed.

"Merry Christmas!" someone would bellow to an unsuspecting Iraqi. The ones who didn't know the story of Christmas soon learned.

"Do you know what Christmas is?" we would ask to the disdainful looks of our captive Muslim audience. "Well, about five hundred years before Muhammad, there was this guy Jesus . . ." and so we would continue with the story of Christmas. It was against policy to speak of religion to the populace, but that night no one cared. It wasn't that we had any interest in spreading Christianity to the masses, it was simply entertaining to annoy them. Most simply stood silently and endured the veiled taunts. Others seemed to display an understanding for our misery, and even sympathy.

"Merry Christmas, mister," a kid said to me from a car window. "I went to the university in England. I know about Christmas," he said with a toothy smile.

"What do you know about Christmas, motherfucker?" Pearson called back without hesitation.

Down the road was an explosion. When they towed the twisted metal remains of the sergeant major's Humvee by, we all stopped and watched. Some family back home was about to receive the worst Christmas present ever. "So this Jesus guy was born, and he was all up in this fucking barn, right?" Pearson continued with his story.

# FIFTEEN

# BAGHDAD ISLAND

BAGHDAD ISLAND? WHAT IS it, a fucking amusement park?"
Boner mocked the lieutenant as we got the briefing. Lieutenant Killearn was a nice enough guy, but he was soft-spoken, and as such was often overwhelmed by the more dominant personalities in the platoon. "Come visit Baghdad Island! You, too, can roll in Third World shit and filth." We all laughed, but no one was eager to check out the world's shittiest theme park. Maghrib had become our home; we had hot chow, occasional showers, and air coolers. We were comfortable for the first time in a year, and the prospect of leaving that for someplace new was daunting.

"All right, dicks, it's only temporary. First AD is getting nailed up there with mortar fire every night, and they don't have any infantry assets to patrol." Sergeant Golder spoke authoritatively, but somehow not reassuringly.

"So it's our job to put our asses out there fucking thirty miles from our sector because *they* can't take care of themselves? Why don't they do their own fucking patrols?" Mitchell had a way of simplifying things beyond the higher-ups' capacity. It was what endeared us to him, and simultaneously earned him so much special, and not so loving, attention from our first sergeant.

Sergeant Golder's only answer came with a harsh glare from a very large man. "We roll day after tomorrow. First Squad is staying here to pull security on the compound."

"Fuck me! Just us? When are we gonna sleep?" Sergeant Jimmy Sims groaned. Sims had shit for luck. In one enlistment, he had managed to not only visit but spend considerable time in such enviable vacation spots as Korea, Bosnia, Croatia, and now Iraq. I was sure he was the one who had cursed us into this mission.

"Second Platoon is giving up guys too. First is on division Quick Reaction Force. What can I tell you? We're on red cycle. Not much we can do about that now, is there?"

"Always on fucking red cycle. I don't think we should answer the phone anymore," someone mumbled. "We're sorry, Alpha Company isn't in right now. Please leave a message and we'll get back to the war whenever it's convenient."

Our last days at the compound passed, as they always did, and we found ourselves seated in the back of five-ton trucks, our rucksacks heaped in piles around us. We carried bivy sacks, ponchos and liners, a spare uniform, and shaving gear. Our pouches were full of extra ammunition, and in my map pouch I had a handful of trashy paperbacks among a rainbow of chemical lights for signaling.

We sat or knelt on our assault packs and faced out through slats in the wooden rails. It always proved to be amazingly uncomfortable this way, but otherwise there was no security. We had no armor escort, and our heavy weapons were relegated to a fifty-caliber machine gun in the front and a Mark 19 grenade launcher in the rear. I covered my mouth to keep the grit out as our funny little caravan lumbered down the busy streets of midmorning.

It was over an hour before we could glimpse our destination. My legs were cramped from being tucked awkwardly beneath me, and I yearned for the chance to take off my sweaty helmet.

"Goddamn Boner! A fucking roller coaster!" Sellers yelled from the front in delight. We all turned to look, and sure enough, a rusty set of tracks climbed into the desert sun, its rails and scaffolding hanging loosely in the wind.

Boner was on his feet, jumping, pointing, and shaking. "Fuck yeah! I'm gonna ride that bitch!"

"You do and you're even crazier than I thought," Pearson answered lackadaisically.

"Shit, I saw this motherfucker attack an entire fraternity with a fire hydrant back at FSU," Brunelle chimed in.

"Yeah, who knew that was a felony, anyway?" Boner had that sly grin on his face that always led to trouble. You couldn't help but like him.

The trucks rolled unceremoniously down a gravel road surrounded on either side by Vietnam-era tents bigger than some
apartments I have lived in. There was a chow hall on the left
and a forty-story tower on the right, but we scarcely noticed.
The thing that stood out were the women. Infantry units don't
have women, but this was no infantry unit, and they were
everywhere. They looked at us, unsure what to make of our
leering smiles and uninhibited stares. We could smell their
hair, hear their laughter, and almost feel their skin.

Baghdad Island, or Catamount Island as First Armored Division had dubbed it after the unit located there, had once
been some kind of resort. Not for the jet-setting superrich, but
more a picnic and campground for the middle class. It was surrounded by water on only three sides, and therefore not an island at all. The moisture allowed for an abundance of flora
that was unprecedented in our collective experience of Iraq. In
parts it was almost triple canopy, and the myriad of ditches
and holes made night patrols hazardous and uncomfortable.
We would return bruised, soaked, and bug-bitten.

A little-known fact in the army is that a soldier's happiness
is directly proportional to the proximity of his chain of command. Our commander and first sergeant had tagged along in
an attempt to get away from the battalion staff. It was a vacation for them, but for the rest of the company, sleeping right
next door to them, it was pure torture.

The women on the "island" only served to make things
worse. In the month that followed they became more comfortable, and eventually they enjoyed the attention, making
sure to walk by us after their showers, in wet clothes with hair

dripping over blue eyes. The male soldiers there didn't harbor the same tolerance to our presence. We were competition in a world where there were already too many single men.

First AD had us patrolling day and night, but that wasn't all. They pulled back their armored vehicles from the perimeter and set us on their line to pull security. We pulled ten-hour days of guard and then left immediately on patrols.

Things were so bad there was nothing to do but take pride in it. When two noncommissioned officers from another company disobeyed orders and married some local Iraqis in a secret ceremony, they were punished by being sent to our platoon. "Worst fucking place in the world, man. Worse even than Leavenworth," someone said.

But we had one comfort. Maybe we didn't have time to sleep because we were patrolling too much, maybe we couldn't talk to the women because the First AD officers got too protective, maybe we couldn't get on the roller coaster for fear of getting shot off it, but our go-home date was set. Our families had been notified and parties were planned. In a little over a month, we would get on the freedom bird and never come back again. The topic never got old, no matter how many days we spent fantasizing about it.

Of course, we had planned the parties before, and so the day that a grizzled old sergeant major swaggered into our barracks, everyone knew what to expect. He was a bear of a man with white hair and wrinkles on his face but not his uniform. He moved confidently among us, his eyes piercing our disheveled minds. In a flash his nine-millimeter Beretta was in his hand. He swung it wildly around, pointing a self-installed laser sight at us. The empty leather holster on his hip creaked as he moved, and the only sound was us breathing.

"You men want to go home, I know. There's lots of politics involved back home, and your senator says he's taking care of you. Well, I'm here to tell you that the army and First Armored Division still need you. You've been extended, and I know you will all make me proud. Any questions?"

Kerr mumbled something about getting new equipment, but was silenced by a shake of the old sergeant's head. After he left, we turned and went back to our cots. Those soldiers who still had someone who cared back home sent letters.

"Honey, I know I told you I'd be home in a month, but things have changed here. Don't be too sad, and don't worry. I'm okay. I love you." Shit, I didn't even know if my letters were even being opened, but habit kept me writing. Someone somewhere had to give a fuck.

Every night on patrol we were mortared or received RPG fire, but our hunt for the culprits proved fruitless. In his desperation to catch someone, our company commander had deemed risk assessments unnecessary. He had picked a sprawling expanse of pasture eleven or twelve kilometers from the compound, and every night, by the same route, we would patrol out and lie there in ambush, shivering in the dew. Even the cherriest privates knew it was bad news, and no matter how we much griped, nothing was done. Routine is the enemy of the infantry. We were just waiting for an attack. Any attempt to deviate from the planned route or ambush site was put to a stop when the commander began sending platoon leaders out with us.

Tonight, the first night after the sergeant major's speech, my squad was spread wide on the dirt road as we trekked into the ambush site like phantoms in the blackness. Along the track home was a small village of ten or so shacks, their mud walls adjoining to house two or three families and their goats. Stray dogs stood guard—against not only humans but the jackals that frequented the island. But we could barely see any of that, because our night-vision equipment had long since been broken. No one had swing arms to mount the PVS-14 monocular, and the army didn't deem fit to provide us with more. The moon was hidden and illumination was near zero. Insects chirped in the night, filling our ears.

The metallic clang of a magazine being slapped home in an AK-47 sent all of us into a hyperalert state. Moments later, machine-gun fire erupted to our right, from the village. Tracers broke the darkness and I dove into a pile of rubble, scraping my knees and elbows before my ears even acknowledged the report of the weapon. The firing stopped.

"Anyone see a muzzle flash?" Brunelle called out.

"I didn't see shit!" someone yelled back. Apparently, no one else had either, and after a few seconds of listening to my own heart beat, I moved up next to Sellers. Kreed saw my movement.

"Crawford, you and Sellers on point! Let's go check out that village. Mears, call Raptor Six and give him a sitrep."

Sellers glanced back at me in the gloom, and I thought I saw him smile.

"You ready?" He didn't wait for an answer, and I didn't give him one. We were up and moving in a low crouch through the night. The brush was thick all around, and we moved as quietly as possible. The rest of the squad followed a little behind, providing overwatch. The mud was thick off the road, and the earth swallowed my boots with every step, making movement slow and difficult.

"Fuck!" Sellers cried out as he began to topple forward. Grabbing the back of his body armor, I yanked him back. In front of us was what can only be described as a canyon, though in reality it was more like a twenty-foot-deep drainage ditch. Either way, there was no way we could pass through it, and I certainly wasn't going to get bottled up in low ground with some unknown enemy looking down on me.

"There's gotta be a bridge or something—follow me," I whispered to Sellers, and I moved off to the right with him in tow. Several times I sank up to my hips in the mud, until I wasn't even sure that my weapon would fire for the grime it had collected.

When we did reach a thin wooden bridge, ten minutes had already passed, and I was sure that any gunman had either repositioned himself for a more successful ambush or simply moved out.

The squad went into a bounding overwatch. One four-man team moved while the other stayed behind cover and gave security to those in the open. When we reached the houses we moved quickly, surprising the unsuspecting residents who had somehow missed our noisy approach.

Women screeched and children wailed. No longer in need of stealth, we moved quickly among them, rounding them up.

Sellers, Pearson, Hightower, and I stacked on the nearest house and prepared to kick in the door.

"Hold up, Sellers!" the lieutenant called out.

"Six element says we can't enter any houses. Not in our rules of engagement."

"What the fuck, sir? How the fuck can we do anything if all they have to do is go inside whenever we get close?" My voice was cracking.

"At ease, Crawford. First AD doesn't want to make any more enemies here, so they don't want us tearing through people's homes. This isn't our sector, remember."

"Fucking bullshit! What—are we supposed to ask this fucker if he shot at us and would he please stop?!" The lieutenant didn't bother to answer. He was busy trying to sort out the situation, doing officer stuff. The women were babbling all together, and occasionally a word we knew was thrown out. The way the women described it, someone had shown up and stolen a generator and their men shot at him. The two men we had found on the scene were squatting on the ground. Brunelle and I walked up to them and they stood, a slight sway in their motions and the smell of whiskey on their breath.

"Holy fuck! Dude, is that the biggest fucking hajji in the world or what?" I said. Brunelle, himself over six feet tall, was dwarfed by the man. Brunelle just nodded. "If this guy gives us any trouble, I'm fucking shooting him, no questions asked."

"No argument from me. You know I'd kill every man, woman, and child in Baghdad if it got me home twenty minutes earlier."

Kreed was still trying to work things out by talking to the

women. "So if they shot at him, where is the rifle? *Boondook?*
*Silah?* . . . Rifle? Weapon?" No answer came from the fidgety
women.

I stood next to Sellers, trying to blend into the darkness. A
young girl ran over to me, squealing like a wild animal. She
grabbed my uniform and tried to climb up it, scratching and
clawing her way to my chest before I pushed her off. She only
returned and intensified her assault, moving awkwardly, eyes
rolling back, some inhuman guttural language invading my ears.

"Is she hurt? Shine your tactical light on her." Sellers looked
concerned from what I could see, and although I didn't think
she was hurt, I too was curious. I reached down with my left
hand and triggered the light. Night became day, and I immediately shut it off as the sudden brightness caused her to shake
uncontrollably and writhe on the ground. When it was off, she
jumped back to her feet and continued to molest me.

"Dude, what are you doing picking on some retarded girl?
Shining your light in her eyes like that. Fucking asshole." Sellers suppressed a laugh as he saw my discomfort. I shook my
head and looked at the girl sadly.

"Fucking retarded and living in Iraq. What could be worse
than that? God must really hate you, little girl." We moved
back onto the road and left the village behind us.

# SIXTEEN

# HANDOUTS

T HE OLD LADY'S HEAD was bowed, and water drizzled down her face and into the weed-covered cracks of the basketball court. At her feet was a pile of crusty and shredded blankets, getting increasingly soaked in the early-morning rain. All around her, refugees walked by, herded into the gymnasium by American and British soldiers, but she stood alone, flanked only by trash littering the ground. Occasionally, she would reach down and attempt to corral the large pile into her arms, but her aged body was too frail to have any effect.

Still no one moved to help. Soldiers leaned against walls, smoking cigarettes and talking. Next to me, a young Brit with bad teeth was telling me about a tour in the Balkans he had just completed. His accent was strong, though, and I understood very little of what he said. He, too, eyed the woman warily, but stood his ground.

Her body was covered in tattoos; lines and dots crisscrossed her forehead, cheeks, and arms. I had seen those markings before, but only on the elderly, evidence of a tradition going extinct. She shivered in the rain and suppressed a hacking cough.

"Well, hell," I muttered with displeasure, and stepped briskly from beneath my shelter into the rain. When I reached her, I slung my weapon behind my back, knelt down, and cradled the mildewed and lice-infested blankets into my arms. The stench made me gag as I lifted them, grunting with their weight.

"How did you even get this shit here, lady?" I asked, repulsed and wishing I had brought my gloves. The woman said nothing. She didn't smile, or nod, or even acknowledge my assistance. She simply shuffled past me in the direction the others had gone. I trailed behind her with the load in my arms.

I stepped over a man with no legs whose friends had abandoned him in the breezeway in order to get in line for food. He weakly grasped my leg as I passed, but I shook my leg, his hand came loose, and he turned for help to someone else.

The gymnasium we entered stunk of the derelicts of a Third World country. There aren't too many worse smells. There was very little room left. Every open space had been claimed. The screeching of children overwhelmed my ears, and the smell made my eyes water and nose crinkle up.

My presence created a small empty space, and I hurriedly dumped the blankets and strode away. The old woman crumpled up, defeated by the effort of walking. The air outside smelled clean and cool, and I did my best to wipe off the germs both imaginary and authentic.

A few days before, we had been relieved in place by soldiers from the First Armored Division. They were finally going to cover down on our sector and let us leave. We were slotted to redeploy within a week: first to Baghdad International Airport, then Balad, then America. Everyone was tense with excitement, and the days moved like molasses. The suspension of patrols was a greatly anticipated moment as well. Finally, we thought, those of us left unscathed might actually make it.

When word came that we had picked up one final mission, the barracks were filled with groans of impatience and disgust.

"During the war, a British jet dropped a five-hundred-pound bomb into a building and it never went off. EOD is going in to disarm and remove it, but first we have to evacuate the area. The residents will be brought to the girls' college. . . ."

"The one by the Amoco?" someone asked, and Lieutenant Killearn nodded his head, then continued.

"We'll provide food and security for these people for twenty-four hours, and then they will be returned to their home in the same buses that brought them. Any questions?"

"How are we supposed to evacuate all these people?"

"Don't worry about that. All we have to do is man the college. First AD is evacuating them. What's more, we'll have other coalition forces attached, mainly the British."

"Will school be in at the college?" Kerr asked with a grin. We all liked flirting with the girls. Unfortunately, the evacuation fell on a weekend and there was no school. Other than that, we had long since gotten past asking numerous questions.

Bombs never seem to fall in the nicer sections of town, or perhaps they are the nicer sections of town because bombs never fall there. The British bomb was no exception. The neighborhood we were taking people from was one of the worst in Baghdad. The refugees we were watching were drug addicts, prostitutes, and the poorest members of a broken society.

When the buses pulled up and our guests began filing out, those who had brought gloves put them on. Most of us just took a step back, unwilling to get close to the disease-infested rabble as they huddled disheveled on one side of the building awaiting instructions. Raindrops echoed off our helmets, and we stood apart, trying not to stare at the lesions and sores that carved their faces. The Iraqis, in turn, looked away for the most part. They were beaten by life, and it amazed me that anyone could live in the condition they were in. A year after we had invaded, these people still had no electricity, no fresh water or food, and they had a higher mortality rate than their ancestors had fifty thousand years prior.

The British soldiers had brought boxes full of toys along with their equivalent of MREs. As the people swarmed in, they were handed one meal, minus the candy and goodies, which mysteriously had disappeared, and the children were handed broken toys, one each. They were undoubtedly donated a world away by some goodwill drive to help impoverished Iraqi children. Within the hour, the Brits grew tired of the monotony and the smell and went back to the safety of the Green Zone, leaving us in charge of food distribution.

Brunelle and I volunteered for the job so we could get out of the rain and take off our helmets. Through an open door, we tossed meals to the people and fought off the fanatical advances of children who wanted more than one broken car or He-Man action figure.

"Hey, Brune! Check this shit out!" I squealed excitedly after rummaging through one of the garbage bags.

"What is it?" he asked over his shoulder as he tossed another meal to someone.

"Cookies! Fucking chocolate chip cookies!" For some reason, the Brits had put all the desserts into huge plastic garbage bags at the back of the supply room.

My mouth was already full, and crumbs littered my chin as I turned to him, box of cookies in hand. Directly in front of me stood an army major, hands on his hips, his eyes burrowing through me in suspicion.

I was caught, literally, with my hand in the cookie jar. I swallowed hard and, seeing there was no escape, extended the box to him.

"Cookie, sir?" I offered with my cheesiest grin. The officer just laughed and walked off, much to my relief. No one wants to get caught eating food that was intended for refugees.

Meanwhile, Brunelle had a Santa puppet on his hand and he was using it to attack children encroaching on our citadel. They squealed with delight and tripped over one another in their flight. After several hours, and a terrible stomachache from too many cookies and mincemeat pies, we were begrudgingly relieved from our position and sent to pull security inside the crowded and sweaty gymnasium.

Someone had tried earlier to throw a box of toys into the center of the room in the hopes that the children would create some sort of mad scramble for them. Indeed, this is what happened: several grown men viciously beat the youngsters with their fists and greedily snatched toys from their tiny hands. The children were less surprised than we were. They moved on to start a makeshift soccer game, using cones as sidelines and a paper cup as the ball.

Occasionally, some officer would walk by and take a proud look around at the great things we were doing in the battle for hearts and minds. But they, like the British, soon tired of this and left us to our babysitting. No one likes to see the not-so-spectacular parts of a war, and we had already lived too many of those moments to give a fuck about anything except ourselves.

When darkness came, the power left and the use of chemical lights proved impossible. Like fireflies swallowed up by night predators, they disappeared into the pockets of the Iraqis one by one until there were only islands of light, and finally, with a flash, there was only blackness. On we sat with our hundreds of neighbors in total darkness. The talk soon died out, and the night was pierced only by the occasional crying child or the moaning whore.

With daybreak came the buses, and we handed out any remaining food for breakfast. One by one, the Iraqis filed out of the gym, leaving only trash and an unbearable odor that I believe is there to this day. A few hours later, we too left, back to our compound and, soon enough, back to America.

# SEVENTEEN

# ONE LUCKY ASS

I DON'T KNOW when I first noticed him. It just seemed like he was always there, chained to a telephone pole on the corner of the Bravo Three intersection across from the old amphitheater. His fur was disheveled and large clumps were falling out, revealing patches of pink skin. Great crusty tears ran down his face, and his ribs could be counted from all the way up the street. Scabs and sores bled out of his neck where the chain rubbed mercilessly, and his hooves were cracked and bloody from the pavement. The neighborhood kids would point at him and joyously cry out, "Saddam! Donkey!" All I knew was that was one miserable creature.

On more than one occasion, I passed him by and thought of shooting him—an animal didn't need to live like that—but I never had the heart. If he could survive the treatment he was already receiving, then maybe he wanted to live more than I thought. We grew accustomed to walking past him and petting his sweaty flank as the flies swarmed around his mouth.

When the night of our last patrol in Baghdad came, we decided to act. The squad moved surreptitiously down a narrow alleyway behind the amphitheater. We came to a stop behind a fountain and allowed the shadows to devour us. I moved forward with Sellers and Brunelle while the rest of the squad hung back for security. Saddam was chained to a post in the ground, the only edible grass just out of reach. He whinnied nervously and shivered as we approached.

"Sssshh, boy, it's okay," Sellers whispered with his finger to his mouth, as if the poor animal could understand either the symbol to whisper or the English language. For whatever reason, though, Saddam quieted down and stood still, his only movements the occasional swish of his tail or shake of his head.

Brunelle reached into one of his ammo pouches and retrieved his Leatherman tool. He worked feverishly on the chain with the wire cutters. The smell was unbearable, and when I unpacked my uniforms a month later in America, I could still smell Saddam shit all over me.

The chain snapped loose and Brunelle gave a victorious whoop. "Run! Get out of here!" we urged him, but Saddam only took a few gingerly steps over to the grass he had undoubtedly been eyeballing for years and began to gorge himself.

A cry went up from a nearby house, and a man clad only in his nightclothes rushed into the dark street yelling curses at us in Arabic. Sellers raised his hand and, with as much strength as he could muster, slapped Saddam on the rump.

"Get on, boy!" he yelled, and Saddam broke into a gallop, his hooves clattering on the empty street. We waylaid the owner until the noise turned into an echo and then faded out altogether. It was the least we could do to give him a decent head start.

Undoubtedly, he was captured shortly thereafter, if not by the same man, then by another who would treat him just as poorly. That really didn't matter, though, either to us or to him. Indifference and apathy had been beaten into the donkey and the Iraqis who had administered the thrashings were no different. They were fickle and didn't give a shit if we came or went or just blew the fuck up. All the same, it was nice to feel we were helping someone for once. Even if that someone was just a run-down old donkey named Saddam.

# EIGHTEEN

# THE LAST TRUE STORY I'LL EVER TELL

THERE WERE TREES EVERYWHERE. That's all I remember thinking: towering green giants smiling down on the world. My foot slid down a little farther on the gas pedal and my dad's old truck responded in turn, roaring up to eighty-five. The windows were up and the air conditioner blew civilization into my face. On the radio was some new band I hadn't even heard of, but it didn't matter. The old paved road I drove on was full of potholes that threatened to suck me in, but that didn't matter either. Everything important was self-contained. My life was complete, better than it had ever been before, and I couldn't even begin to ruin it by putting it into words.

My wife sat next to me, red hair cradling her doll face as her lips mouthed the words to a song I hadn't heard before. She looked at me, and her eyes twinkled. They were hazel today; yesterday I had thought they were green; it all depended on her mood, I guess. She smiled and put her hand on top of mine. The vibration of the gearshift coursed like an electrical current between us when we touched, and it made my heart tingle.

"God, I missed you so much," I whispered barely audibly over the other noises that cycloned around us.

"I know, baby, I missed you too." My wife put her arm under mine and pulled herself close, her head resting warmly on my shoulder. Her eyes looked through the bug-covered windshield at the road ahead as she wondered where we were going. My own were clouded by tears of happiness. When I was a boy I wasn't allowed to cry, but I guess crying from sheer joy is acceptable.

Stephanie may have wondered where we were going on this windy stretch of blacktop. I had driven this road a thousand times in my childhood and had dreamed of it a thousand more while I was in Iraq. I was home.

We were going into my hometown, a tiny speck of a city south of Jacksonville. Our only claim to fame was the annual Blue Crab Festival. Every Memorial Day, hundreds of thousands of tourists flock to Palatka for the fresh seafood, entertainment, and most important, the beer tent. Tourists, stomachs full from too many crustaceans and arms tired from carrying pieces of carved driftwood and homemade jam, would stop by for one drink and spend the rest of the evening and their wallets there.

Parking was hard to find that time of year, but locals always have tricks, and I was no different. I pulled into the darkened parking lot of Saint Monica's Catholic Church. The engine sputtered to a stop, an occasional clanking continuing as we gathered our effects and stepped out into the shadows behind old Father Joe's house. No tow truck would venture here unless he wanted an earful from the elderly Irish priest.

I reached out in the darkness and found a loving hand. Together we ventured out into the bustling avenue. The craft stores that ventured for a mile in either direction were mostly closed. It was near ten at night, and the remaining food for sale had been swimming in grease all day like tadpoles in a mud puddle. Next to the mural of Billy Graham we turned east toward the riverfront. As we walked, I saw familiar faces. We smiled and nodded to each other—some kid I rode a bus with, another who had suffered through high school trigonometry with me. There was no reason to say hi. Nothing ever changed in my hometown; there was nothing new to talk about.

My wife was from the North. Well, not strictly. Most people don't consider DC to be particularly up there, but when you grow up in Florida, if it snows, it's the North. I looked over at my angel and saw she was gawking, mouth half open, at my battered town and its residents. Most of the tourists go home fairly early, and the locals who spend their days hiding in shantytowns come out like roaches. It wasn't her first visit to Palatka, but it was her first Blue Crab Festival, and that takes some getting used to. People staggered by with no teeth. A man with a hunchback talked to his one-armed girlfriend. A policeman sat sipping a beer and flirted with a seventeen-year-old dropout. I couldn't help broadening my smile and taking a deep breath of stale beer and fried food. For a second I watched it all fade away into the slums, tans, and reek of Baghdad. Smoke and rotten meat tickled my nose. I shook my head. That couldn't happen; I was home.

"John Fucking Crawford!" I swiveled around on my heels and into a bear hug from Kris.

"Kris, what's up?"

He gave Stephanie a hug too. They had met at the wedding, although I wasn't sure that she approved of my Palatka friends. They were all hard-partying guys, and Kris stood out among them, as I had once.

"Where's everyone at?"

"In the beer tent. C'mon, we saved you a seat."

The beer tent was the unequivocal center of the world during Blue Crab. In reality, the whole festival was an excuse to erect a circus tent full of beer-dispensing vixens and tired bands playing tired songs.

The night felt different, though—everything was more colorful and alive. Kris led me to the table where Quint and Joe sat with their wives. They both laughed out loud and gave me hugs when I approached. I laughed, uncomfortable with all the attention, but it sure was good to see them. Quint had been the popular one in school and all the girls had craved his attention. His wife, Amanda, perched on his shoulder and fed off his smile. She scarcely acknowledged the rest of us. If I was unsure how Stephanie felt about my friends, there was no doubt how Amanda viewed Quint's friends.

Next to them were Joe and Jamila. The three of us were

closer than the rest because we had gone to Florida State at the same time. Joe was the smartest of us, but still managed to pull off hanging with us. He met Jamila at a bar in Tallahassee; I had been there when they met. Joe had told me to stay away, that she was his the moment they met, and a few years later they were married and Joe was still entranced with her.

There were plenty of hugs and smiles around, and a scantily clad blonde with a soft keg attached to her back came around and filled all our beers for a dollar.

"So I hear you guys just got back from Europe?" I started to say, provoking a long, partially boring tale of exotic cities and cultures. I wanted to catch up on a year and a half's worth of gossip, but the rest of the table was more interested in watching Tony's band play. I hadn't heard them in years, and they had gotten really good.

The beer kept coming like a horror-movie villain, always right behind you. Life was good, my friends were there, my wife sat next to me, her hand resting on my thigh under the table as we smiled at everyone and laughed. We downed drink after drink and talked about the time I nearly flipped my first truck not twenty minutes after it was bought.

We decided to go to Quint's farm the next day and do some shooting, sans the women. Tony's band was kicking, and people were getting up to dance or crowd the stage. The place was full of gleeful noises, young girls giggled and flirted, and old men told fish stories. Lovers whispered and laughed around us. I looked around and felt like pumping my fist in the air. I was home.

"So . . . we spent the last summer in Europe and we told you about that. Tell us about your summer, John?" Joe asked, his eyes on mine, trying to read me.

"Summer, my ass. It fucking sucked."

"Yeah, whatever. C'mon, man, what was it like?" Kris jumped in.

"Tell us a war story." Quint threw in "Did you shoot anyone?" The rest of the table cheered in agreement and leaned forward over their plastic cups in anticipation. Even my wife looked at me expectantly. I had always been a storyteller, and they were excited to hear what yarn I would give them about this one.

"You guys don't want to hear a war story. None of them make any fucking sense. I'll tell you guys all you want tomorrow." But they wouldn't give up. They badgered, pestered, and hounded me until they saw me breaking.

I leaned over and took a cigarette from Quint's pack, which rested in the center of the table.

"Lemme get a cigarette."

"I suppose you want a light too? Next you'll be taking the fillings outta my fucking teeth." Everyone laughed at Quint's joke except me.

I arrived in An Nasiriyah on March 22. Third Infantry Division had come through an hour earlier and smoldering bodies blackened the sides of the road. In their rush north, the invaders had simply blown through whatever opposition they had met, but bypassed much of the city. We came in with the First Marine Expeditionary Force and were immediately bogged down by heavy fighting. The marines were taking heavy casualties inside the city, while my platoon sat just outside city

limits guarding an ammunition supply point that had previously belonged to the Eleventh Iraqi Infantry Division. They
had popped smoke at the first sign of American armor. The
eggs and flour were still damp on the kitchen counter. Human
shit crawled out of the corners to get underneath your boots.
No one really noticed it very much, though; we were all pre-
occupied with staring openmouthed at the cache of weapons
we had found. There were warehouses literally full of rifles,
grenades, missiles, mortars, and rocket-propelled grenades. It
was one of those sights that overwhelm the mind by just going
on as far as the eye can see.

The area we had to secure was too big for one platoon,
and we spent most of the time as a quick reactionary force
speeding down dusty roads after looters or guerrilla soldiers
sneaking in for resupply. We did this for about a week, just
high-speed chases through the desert after rag-clad hajjis. The
modern buildings of Nasiriyah loomed on one horizon, while
Abraham's temple reached toward the sky in the other direction. We were in the biblical city of Ur, and I remember being
impressed with that. It was still very early in the war.

The place was a slum, though. Bedouins herded goats past
us, paying no more attention to us than we did them. Mud-
brick houses broke up the skyline. Donkey carts and starving
people milled about, rummaging through the belongings of
the dead. It was a sight one would expect to find after stepping
out of a time machine. Aside from the very occasional beat-up
taxicab, it was like looking at a portrait from five thousand
years ago. The smell was what I remember most. Burned human flesh combined with diesel and shit. There were bodies all

over the place, and although we ran into a few live ones, most of the combatants had long ago left. Some of the guys took pictures, but that wasn't for me. I had no urge to reminisce later over photos of meat on the ground.

We were smack dab in the center of the fertile crescent, except it wasn't nearly as fertile as I had imagined. On one side of the road there were fields of super-green crops, and then, like a dog at the end of its leash, they would stop and turn into lifeless desert. There was no happy reception from the Iraqis. We were greeted with indifference. No one clapped or waved flags. They just stared at us and waited for us to leave. We raided nearby houses and buildings looking for soldiers hiding there. We were excited, ready to get things over with and go home. We were itching. It had been more than two months since any of us had talked to loved ones or received any mail. We were on two meals a day plus water ration, and on top of that we were eating sand, drinking sand. Sand was in every orifice of our bodies. At some point, you begin to imagine that you're made of sand. It gets into you, the desert, not physically, but really into your soul until you're just pissed off.

There was a complex of bunkers to our north, and my squad moved out one morning to clear them. They were empty, but in one room we came upon a large map overlay. Twice as tall as me and from one corner of the room to the other, it marked every Iraqi unit position south of the Tigris River. We called it in, and the commander told us to take it and Charlie mike—continue mission.

There was nothing else of interest, and before long we returned, drenched in sweat, to the perimeter. The company commander took one look at that map and decided that it needed to be taken to the division headquarters in what is now Tallil Air Force Base. Back then it was just a mechanized battalion, some Special Forces guys, and a few rear-echelon motherfuckers. Regardless, our company commander thought he would get all sorts of kudos for the map *he* had found, so he loaded up in another Humvee with a goofy first lieutenant who looked like he couldn't run a Boy Scout troop, and together we went toward Tallil. They were moving ahead of us, and the sun was slowly painting the desert red as it set.

Staff Sergeant Connel was driving, Specialist Ramirez was in the back with a 240 golf machine gun, and I rode in the passenger seat with my M-249 squad automatic weapon as flank security. The Humvees we drove in were unarmored. You could throw a rock through them if you had a good enough arm, and hell, we didn't even have doors on. There we were, driving thirty-five miles an hour through an area that later that night would be nicknamed Ambush Alley because a young maintenance female got taken prisoner. Best way to earn medals in the army, after all—get lost or be an officer. Do both at the same time and you might even get a high school named after you.

On the right side of the road was the desert. The huts and hovels had sheets flapping in front of the door, light from kerosene lanterns peeking out. Chickens and goats ran free, while young girls and old ladies tried to finish up the daily chores before darkness fell. They stepped mindlessly over the bodies, washing clothes and maintaining the facade that they lived in complete normalcy.

The men, meanwhile, were content to sit on their stoops smoking cigarettes and drinking beer. The little boys emulated them by taking it easy as well. They frolicked about, skipping among the stones. There was no danger in the air, so it was with a total lack of fear that I noticed a group of little boys playing on the left side of the road. There were three, all about eight or nine years old. They stood knee deep in crops, their ragged clothes blowing in the wind around their emaciated bodies. I was about to wave cordially when the center one reached up and pointed his finger at the commander's Humvee in front of us. The sun was setting behind them, and as we rolled up, that finger became the front sight post of an AK-47. Anyone who has ever seen one knows there's nothing else to mistake it for with its thick metal triangle; there's no other rifle in the world that looks like that.

"Fuck!" I yelled to no one.

"He's got a fucking AK!" I yelled again.

It was on the opposite side of the vehicle from me, so there was little I could do except shout a warning. Sergeant Connel slammed on the brakes. The tires squealed and struggled against the pavement, and our screeching halt came with a black rubbery smell catching up with us. Ramirez, on the machine gun in the back, never even got to point in that direction. The sudden stop caused him to fly forward halfway over the cab, his gun banging noisily on the hood.

Connel's rifle sling was snagged on something in the vehicle, and despite his tugs and frantic curses he couldn't free it. Without doors or seat belts, I slid easily out of the Humvee and had my feet in the dirt before the stop was even complete.

I slammed my saw onto the hood with a clank. The bipod legs on my weapon were still up and in the locked position, but the boys weren't very far away, so accuracy wasn't too much of a problem.

Our sudden stop had caused quite a commotion, and all three boys were looking at us now. Their eyes wide with wonder. The one holding the rifle slowly turned it toward me. It seemed so slow the way he moved, but I suppose that was just the way I remember everything happening. My safety was already off, and I had him in the middle of my sight picture.

*Why don't they run?* Most likely they didn't realize that in a tenth of a second their bodies would be ripped apart, shredded by a hundred bullets manufactured a world away in Cleveland or somewhere. They couldn't have known that that very night the dogs that scavenged the desert would be tearing out their entrails and that they would be unrecognizable to the morning.

I held my breath and steadied on the hood of that vehicle as best I could. They were silhouetted black against the sunset, and I could clearly see the entire barrel assembly of the rifle with a thirty-round magazine locked into the bottom. The muzzle was almost on me, and I had already hesitated too long. While they stood on the swelling bloody sun, I applied pressure to the trigger.

I don't know if that was before or after I realized that the rest of the rifle was missing. The trigger was gone, as was the buttstock and bolt. Someone had killed a hajji there the day before and just run over his rifle with their track, rendering it useless. That kid couldn't have shot spitballs through it even if he had wanted to.

No one at the table said a word; our circle had become a pool of awkward silence. Stephanie squeezed my leg under the table in support, but I didn't move.

"It's no big deal, man, you can just tell us a story some other time," Joe said reassuringly. The table began to resurrect; cups were refilled, cigarettes lit. Tony's band had stopped playing and they were now introducing all the members. The chattering in the background was coming back, growling into a great screeching howl. I wanted to stay and talk, but couldn't. After a few more halfhearted attempts to laugh, we left.

My wife and I were silent as we passed the church on our way back to the car. I remembered being an altar boy when I was, as Father Joe described me, "a wee lad." He used to place this oversized Bible on my head and read from it to the congregation as if I were some form of human lectern. The churchgoers would snicker, incensing me, but I was just a little boy then. I was a man now, and I was fairly sure that book wouldn't fit on my head anymore. What did it matter, though? I was home.

A crashing boom broke the night air and I jumped up on my cot with a start. It took me a moment to realize where I was. Pearson and Hightower were already up, throwing on body armor and grabbing weapons to defend the perimeter. I wiped sleep from my eyes. I had been dreaming, nothing more. It was just a vision of what home could or should be.

What I'm about to write is true. Utterly true. The first thing I wrote for this book was a fiction short story I wrote while still in Iraq. It was all about returning home and finding myself in a world where no one understood my experience, but they were all there to support me. My wife was on my arm, telling me that no matter what she loved me. We would have children soon, and the rest of my life would be wonderful. I was wiser in that story than I am now. Like Joseph Campbell's hero with a thousand faces, I returned victorious. I told tales of my exploits and people listened. They cared.

It wasn't until I got back that truth engulfed me like a storm cloud. Dreams and truth are never intertwined.

I spent a few months drifting around friends' houses, from one couch to the next. When I finally got enough money to get an apartment again, I kept getting kicked out.

I was evicted from one place I was renting because I have a dog, a big one. He sleeps with me at night when I'm drunk and can't understand why I'm alone. Dogs don't turn their backs on you, that's another truth. I moved five times in five months.

Most days I was sick. It was a lingering, wasting sickness that comes only when you have nothing left. There are people out there who really don't know why they get up in the morning; it's sad, and that's how you know it's true.

In my dream, my wife never told me that things would have been better off if I had just never come home. In reality, I agree with her.

This is a true story. You can tell because it makes your stomach turn. I am home now, and I will never again write a true story.

# EPILOGUE

Private Dwight had been walking in a sandstorm when he tripped and accidentally pulled the charging handle on his M-16. After a few more steps he fell again, disengaging the safety and firing one round directly into the top of his boot and through his foot. None of us really believed that story, but that didn't really matter. There were powder burns on the leather and a star-shaped hole where discharge gases had exited the muzzle. A tiny bit of blood trickled out. By the time Sergeant Gilleon found him, Dwight was yelling, "Oh Lawd! I'm dyin'! My gran'ma gon' be soo disappointed!"

People deal with stress and fear in different ways. That was just Dwight's way. Sergeant Stanley used to sit on the balcony outside his room and chain-smoke in between patrols. It was so common to see him, hands shaking, puffing away at any time of day or night that we began to call him Smoky. Eventually it got so bad that he was taken off the line and put in charge of training an Iraqi National Guard platoon.

Boner, on the other hand, just sat up on the roof away from the prying eyes of the officers, in a kiddie pool filled with brown water drinking Turkish beer. Operation Splish-Splash was a great way to get relaxed, he would say with a slur, but all he ever seemed to get was a sunburn and a headache.

We all did things at one time or another that defied logic. Sometimes you start to feel like someone is just in your head screaming at the top of his lungs so that you can't think. Whatever stops, or at least muffles it, is worth a try. This book is a direct result of my attempts to stop the screaming.

Our room in the Republican Guard barracks had once been used as family quarters. There was a main room, probably twelve feet by eight feet. In it slept Kreed, Brunelle, Whigham, Whittaker, and Sellers. The other room was probably half as long and that was where Pearson, Farmer, and I slept. As time changed so did some of the squad members. Farmer was replaced by Hightower, and somewhere along the way Private Ortega showed up, but I don't remember when or why. All I know is that if you didn't watch him, he'd steal your shit right out from under you.

In between the two sleeping quarters was a small side room. Originally designed as a kitchen, it was now dark, smelly, and inhabited by a vicious rat that enjoyed chewing on Global

Positioning Systems and could jump and bite at the same time when cornered late at night in the bathroom. We had stacked the room full of A-Bags and rucksacks immediately upon our arrival, and it took a certain kind of courage just to venture into the darkness to retrieve your extra neck gaiter or Gore-Tex.

One slow morning, I was lying on my cot listening to some terrible mixed CD of Sellers's and staring at our storage closet when I just got up and began tearing through it. I didn't have anything other than a vague reasoning behind it. The clutter inside that darkened recess had become too much for me to bear.

Things hadn't gotten particularly bad at that point, and it's not like I was depressed or consciously worried. Still, the rumblings of discontent had begun to boil. The phone was picked up just a little less often at home. I found myself looking with greater disdain on the Iraqis we had come to liberate. I lived for any excuse to deliver violence on them. This isn't a confession; this is life.

Out came the cooler, still full of stale water from our third of July party. I kicked it into the bathroom where it drained through a rusty grate. The duffel bags and rucksacks were next. Nine of each, tossed throughout the room. The other guys watched my fit, perhaps a bit concerned. "We can use it as a jack-off room. Watch porn in there," I pointed out quickly to make sure they didn't think I was losing my mind. That explanation more than appeased them. The bathroom was the only place with privacy, and there wasn't much room for answering the bone-a-phone in there.

I tore out the rotted cabinets, scratching my hands on nails and scattering roaches. The wood went out the window and eventually into a burn pile. I swept, mopped, arranged all the gear against a wall and, finally, acquired a light. When it was all done, I wheeled in an old office chair and closed the door. Silence; I was alone.

I'd always enjoyed writing, and had even carried English as a second major at Florida State for a while until, figuring there wasn't much in the way of job opportunities there, I dropped it. But sitting there alone in that room, something overtook me, tedium mixed with a need to make something, to look at it and feel as if my mind had purged itself of its demons. All I know was that within minutes I was huddled over Pearson's laptop typing out a story and listening to Pink Floyd's *Dark Side of the Moon*.

> *And all you touch and all you see,*
>   *is all your life will ever be.*

The story was about something that had happened in Nasiriyah. I imagined that I was home with my wife and friends telling them about the war. The scenes in that story had been going through my head for weeks. We thought our Go Home Date was fast approaching, and I was working it all out in my head; the conversations and questions that would occur. I would sit up on the roof at night and imagine the looks of awe on their faces. I was writing it for me, to work out the finer details of their reactions in my fantasy.

The door slammed in the other room, and there were loud voices. I pushed the Stop button and could hear Kreed doing introductions. Sellers's voice boomed, and through the flimsy Iraqi walls I could make out what was going on. Two journalists had joined us for the day, embedded for twenty-four hours. A documentary filmmaker and a writer who was assisting with the camera equipment and working on a book about the occupation.

The filmmaker was passing on his credentials: "Remember the guy out in California that stole the tank and went on a rampage on the freeway before the cops killed him? I did a documentary on him." That was cool; I'd seen that video on every *Wildest Police Chases* show ever made.

KREED STUCK his head in my retreat as the writer looked over his shoulder. "This here's Crawford in the jack-off room." I gave him a dirty look. When I had been in the 101st we used to do media training with fake reporters asking rigged questions. You either said, "I'm not sure I understand the question, sir, but if you'll follow me I can escort you to my platoon leader" or you just ignored them.

"How's it going?" he asked with a broad smile as he stepped through the door. He looked confident, but behind it he had the wariness of someone who has just cornered a dog. I didn't realize why until much later when I saw the footage of that day. My eyes weren't just empty, they were downright mean. I wasn't myself then.

He eyed my CD player suspiciously. The latch was broken and it was held together by frayed duct tape. No sound was coming from the headphones and I believe he was on to my ruse.

"Are you writing something? Can I read it?" I shrugged and turned the screen his way. He read for a few minutes before being summoned back into the other room to work a camera for an interview; a portrait of Sellers hamming it up.

On patrol that afternoon, he eased up next to me, we talked for a few minutes about literature and politics, and when he asked if I could get him a copy of my story, I said, "Sure." The command post had a printer, so it was no real problem. He left with what would become the final chapter of this book and my email address.

We kept in contact. I sent him a few more stories, and he sent us some of the raunchiest pornography I have yet to see.

WHITTAKER WAS A good guy, as nice as you could get, but damnit if he wasn't a sleeper. Brunelle told me that during the invasion, as we had crossed the berm into Iraq no less, he had looked over and seen Preacher's head down on his chest, bobbing along with the bumps in the road.

"Wake up motherfucker!" he yelled with a slap of his hand to Whit's Kevlar.

"What! Uh . . . I was praying."

Some people just fall asleep easier than others, so it was no real surprise to us when word came that the sergeant major had been checking the observation posts on the roof of our building and caught Whittaker catching some Z's up there around two in the morning. Now if your squad leader catches you sleeping, you're liable to get a stern talking-to and maybe some extra guard time, but when a sergeant major gets you, man, you're fucked.

So Preacher got demoted from specialist back to private first class, and understandably he was upset. Later in the week Kreed came to me and pulled me aside.

"Crawford, I gotta talk to you about Whit."

"Yeah, what's up?"

"Look, he's all fucked up about getting demoted and he's not handling it well. I talked to him for a while and he wants to move a cot into the storage room and sleep in there."

"What the fuck for? The rest of us sleep just fine out here, why should he get his own room?"

"Look, I know you're the one who cleaned it out, and you use it the most, so I'm asking, not ordering you. He won't move in there unless you give him the okay." I relented and Whittaker moved into the old storage closet. Later Kreed told me how pissed he was. He didn't think I'd give in so easily. Not only did I lose my writing space, but we all lost the jack-off room.

IT WAS RAINING the day I stepped off the plane and into a chilly Georgia morning. The line of soldiers, heads down, struggled underneath the weight of their gear across the tarmac and into a long, low building full of Red Cross coffee and doughnuts. Along the way a general stood shaking hands and exchanging salutes with the returning soldiers. Next to him, a young lieutenant shivered as he held an umbrella out at arm's length over the general. Neither had combat patches on their uniforms, and I splashed by without saluting or shaking hands.

The first time I had been at that airport, there had been banners and flags, family members waving fervently at the departing plane. This time the weather, I guess, had kept them home, and the gray sky was the only real witness to our return. Clouds or no, the "freedom bird" had landed and our war was over; we were home.

That night, in the same dilapidated World War II barracks that we had deployed from an eternity before, I didn't sleep. I thought it was because of the Christmas-morning-like tremble in the air. In reality, I had become addicted to Valium in Baghdad and was going through withdrawal. Sitting alone on my bunk in the darkness, I felt a wave of nausea approaching. That sick feeling hasn't entirely gone away yet.

A week later someone gave a speech, and bags full of coupons for free double cheeseburgers and oil changes were handed out. (Most of the good freebies had already been plundered by seventeen-year-old enlistees who hadn't yet been to basic training.) And with a wave good-bye and a pat on the back, we were civilians again. I heard there was a parade a few months later, but I was too drunk to go, and it wasn't on television.

While many in my platoon had relatively easy transitions, within days, I found myself kept from homelessness only by the hospitality of a friend with a sofa. It was like being at a party and going to the restroom for fifteen months and then trying to rejoin the conversation. Everyone and everything had changed without asking me first.

I took solace in becoming the kind of self-deprecating drunk who shows up at parties naked and wonders why everyone reacts the way they do. The sequence of events that followed culminated in my waking up on the dingy bathroom floor of an even dingier one-bedroom apartment devoid of furniture, except for a couch pulled from a Dumpster early one rainy morning before the garbage man could claim it. In that bathroom, fighting off sickness from the year's excess, with my dog eyeing me and wondering if a coup d'état would be necessary to ensure his continued food supply, I did some soul-searching.

I didn't find a whole lot. I don't have nightmares, or see faces. When there is a flash outside my window at night I know it's just lightning and not a flare or explosion. I can even drive without cringing at the slightest pile of rubble along the roadside in anticipation of an ear-rending explosion and shrapnel tearing through my flesh. I rarely get into fights with people who I imagine are "eyeballing me." I actually adjusted quite well.

It certainly could have been worse. One of my buddies got locked up in an institution by the police for being a danger to himself. Another woke up in the hospital with no memory of the beating he received from those same police—not for being a danger to himself, but to everyone else. One guy got a brain infection and wakes up every morning expecting to be in Iraq. Two more are in Afghanistan, having re-upped rather than deal with being home. Five more went back to Baghdad as private security guards. Their consensus on how it is a second time around: still hot and nasty.

The ones who are still around here I don't see as much as I used to; that doesn't come as much of a surprise. Too many things have happened since we got back a little over a year ago. Busy schedules and girls have gotten in the way. Classes have to be attended, jobs worked; life goes on.

War stories end when the battle is over or when the soldier comes home. In real life, there are no moments amid smoldering hilltops for tranquil introspection. When the war is over, you pick up your gear, walk down the hill and back into the world.

ABOUT THE AUTHOR

John Crawford was newly married and two credits away from completing a B.A. in anthropology at Florida State University when he was sent to Iraq. He thought he was finished with his soldiering days after completing a three-year stint with the army's famed 101st Airborne Division, and his National Guard service was little more than an afterthought. Crawford and his National Guard unit shipped out to Kuwait in February 2003, and crossed into Iraq on the first day of the invasion. Baghdad fell more quickly than anyone had planned, and while most of the soldiers involved with the invasion were sent home, Crawford's National Guard unit was attached to another division and stayed in Baghdad to patrol the city for more than a year. Crawford now lives in Florida, where he is completing his degree and writing. He no longer has any affiliation with the army.